GRACEFUL
EXITS

GRACEFUL EXITS

How Great Beings Die

DEATH STORIES OF
TIBETAN, HINDU & ZEN MASTERS

Compiled and edited by Sushila Blackman

WEATHERHILL
New York • Tokyo

First edition, 1997

Published by Weatherhill, Inc.
568 Broadway, Suite 705
New York, New York 10012

Library of Congress Cataloging-in-Publication Data
   Graceful exits: how great beings die: death stories of Tibetan, Hindu, & Zen
     masters / compiled and edited by Sushila Blackman.—1st ed.
       p.   cm.
    ISBN 0-8348-0391-7 (soft: alk. paper)
     1. Death—Religious aspects—Buddhism. 2. Death—Religious aspects—
Hinduism. 3. Buddhism—Doctrines. 4. Hinduism—Doctrines.
I. Blackman, Sushila.
BQ4487.G43 1997
294.3'423—dc21   97-2451
                                                   CIP

CONTENTS

To Bhagawan Nityananda, Baba Muktananda,
and Gurumayi Chidvilasananda,
the living embodiment of the Siddha lineage.

INTRODUCTION

In that marvelous Indian epic poem, the *Mahabharata,* the sage Yudhisthira is asked: "Of all things in life, what is the most amazing?" Yudhisthira answers: "That a man, seeing others die all around him, never thinks that he will die."

☙　☙

Two thousand years later, people still circumambulate the reality of their own death. In a recent *New York Times* article, infectious disease specialist Dr. Jack B. Weissman remarked, "What strikes me about our system is that more people are afraid of how they are going to die than the fact that they are going to die." When we do think of dying, we are more often concerned with how to avoid the pain and suffering that may accompany our death than we are with really confronting the meaning of death and how to approach it. We are in dire need of role models, people to show us how to face leaving this world gracefully and to place death in its proper perspective. For this it is natural to turn to those most experienced in dealing with death (and with life): spiritual masters.

The Tibetan Buddhist, Zen Buddhist, and Hindu or Yogic traditions that are the focus of this book are deeply linked. One of these links is the extraordinary importance they place on the act of dying. To understand why, we need look no further than the principles of karma and reincarnation, which have been intricately woven into the fabric of life in the East since ancient times.

KARMA AND REBIRTH

According to the law of karma, all beings experience the consequences of their actions—both mental and physical. The myriad desires and fears of each lifetime compel us to keep returning to earthly life to experience the fruits of our previous actions, whether bitter or sweet. Just as we bring the impressions from our waking life into our dreams, so the residual impressions of our actions in this lifetime accompany us to the next. The kind of life we come back into is determined, in large part, by how we live our present life. The masters from the East maintain that to live righteously, let alone to die well, one must act without any personal attachment to one's actions. To be delivered from the fear of death and the certainty of rebirth, one must act without desire, without a personal agenda, and without attachment to results.

Hindus maintain that until the individual soul (*jiva*) merges with the Absolute, the Self of all, it continues to be reborn. The Buddha also endorsed the traditional Indian view that humans are trapped in an endless cycle of lives, known as *samsara*, characterized by *dukkha*, or suffering. According to his teachings, there is no easy escape from this fate because our karma—the consequences of our actions—survives the death of the body to condition a new physical existence. The Buddha did not teach

8

that the individual is reborn; he insisted that all things are subject to the law of mutability or impermanence (known in Buddhism as *anicca*) and that there is no such thing as a personal identity or soul, a doctrine known as *anatta* or "no-self." However, karma—which can be understood as a package of energy containing both negative and positive charges—is transferrable from one life to the next.

Belief in reincarnation and the cycle of rebirth is not unique to the Buddhists and Hindus. For example, an ancient Egyptian hermetic text fragment states that "the soul passes from form to form, and the mansions of her pilgrimages are manifold." There is also at least one passage in the Bible that suggests Jesus may have believed in reincarnation. In Matthew 17:13, Christ reveals his divine form to his three closest disciples, and then tells them that his precursor, John the Baptist, is actually an incarnation of the prophet Elijah. Origen, a prominent patriarch of the early Christian church, described rebirth in his *De Principiis*:

> The soul has neither beginning nor end... Every soul comes to this world strengthened by the victories or weakened by the defeats of its previous life. Its place in this world as a vessel appointed to honor or dishonor is determined by its previous merits.

Thus the early Christians, like their master, appear to have accepted reincarnation, but the concept was suppressed by the Emperor Justinian's Council of Constantinople in 538 AD. In the Jewish mystical tradition of the Middle Ages, the notion of a preexisting soul developed over time into the idea of reincarnation. According to David Chidester in his book *Patterns of Transcendence*, the Kabbalistic concept of *gilgul* (metempsychosis) came to signify a process whereby souls were continuously reborn until—through meditation, prayer, and conscientious ritual observance—they were purified of all sin and eventually restored to God.

Recently documented incidents also point toward the authenticity of reincarnation: children returning to cities where they lived in previous lives and identifying family members; the selection of *tulkus* (reincarnated lamas) from a written list of attributes left by the previous incarnation; and the spontaneous past-life regression experiences of many patients while under hypnosis by medical doctors, such as those Dr. Brian Weiss recounts in his book *Many Lives, Many Masters*. Such data are eroding the objections of even hardened skeptics and nudging us to revamp our understanding of who we are. As Stephen Levine so marvelously puts it in his book *Who Dies?* it is time for us to perceive ourselves "as spiritual beings with physical experiences rather than as physical beings with spiritual experiences." This is how great beings perceive themselves, and how, to our great fortune, they perceive us as well.

THE PINNACLE OF HUMAN LIFE

If there is something that continues into another life, what is the nature of that something? The masters refer to this "something" by different names. Buddhist practitioners have called it a "psychospiritual substratum" or "a stream of existence-energy," while Hindus or followers of yoga refer to it as the *atman*, or soul. They concur on one crucial point, however: that the goal of life for every man and woman is liberation—not to leave any residual impressions at all.

Liberation from the cycle of birth-and-death may sound like an abstruse concept that does not touch us immediately. But in truth, to leap clear of birth-and-death is the final object of human life. In Zen it is called the supreme problem, the most pressing of all problems. The pinnacle of a human life is to die and not to be reborn. This most sublime and remarkable of ends is referred to as self-realization, final liberation, or nirvana (a term that suggests the blowing out of the fire of passions). And, in what is sometimes called the best-kept secret of the East, we learn that we don't have to wait until we die to attain this final goal. The cycle of birth and death can be broken now. Nirvana, or self-realization, can be attained within this lifetime.

When the Taoist philosopher Chuang-tzu was asked why Master Wang Tai was so extraordinary, he replied: "Life and death are revered as great moments of change, yet to him they are as no change at all. Heaven and Earth may topple over and collapse around him, yet he would remain without a stir. His mind is pure and flawless, therefore he does not share the same fate as the things around him." Once one knows one's true nature, the death of the physical body becomes irrelevant—death is no longer real. The masters reassure us that this process of self-realization or nirvana is not an annihilation, not something to fear. They liken the final state to the merging of a raindrop into the ocean—existence remains, but one's limitations and sense of separateness dissolve.

Once a person has broken through to this final state, reincarnation is no longer a necessity. No continuing factor, linking one incarnation with another, remains. This does not mean that the liberated being never returns—some do, out of compassion for mankind. The Hindu tradition speaks of voluntary reincarnations, called *vyutthana*, by fully enlightened masters who return to earthly life even after *maya* (illusion) and the operation of karma has ceased to bind them. Similarly, Buddhists believe that bodhisattvas—the "enlightened beings" who are the embodiment of compassion—will defer their own final liberation, returning to assist all sentient beings in their struggle toward realization.

While many of us have been taught to live well now because of consequences—the rewards of heaven, for example—the masters teach us that this "carrot" must be transcended completely. Great masters live well, not for anticipated personal gain, but for the love of God. Their lives are full of selfless service, because they understand that we are all one.

The Buddha declared that all men could test his path of non-attachment for themselves. While many of us around the world today contemplate this goal, aspire to it, and even actively pursue it, in our heart-of-hearts we often harbor doubts that it is actually within our reach. The masters in this book show us—by their own example—that it is. Some of them attained realization while alive; others attained the final state at death. They are our role models, in life and in death. By extracting and savoring their subtle presence from these stories, we can renew daily our commitment to the goal. We need only to pause a little and dip into the unending river of their grace.

LEAVING THE BODY

"Everyone wants to know the details of dying, though few are willing to say so." So begins Sherwin Nuland's recent bestseller

How We Die. Over the past few years, I have found in myself a growing curiosity about the details of how great beings die. This curiosity, however, is about the subtle rather than the physical aspects. For me, the questions are more about the unseen issues, the mysteries. For example, one question seekers frequently ask is why do self-realized beings, who have transcended the body, have physical pain and suffering at all? When Ramakrishna, one of India's greatest saints, was dying of throat cancer, someone asked him how he would explain this. He answered that where there is form, there is pain, there is suffering. With such self-realized masters, however, we see that while the external self may experience the ravaging effects of a disease, the inner self—the self they are most deeply connected to—is totally at peace.

For a master, death is not death but liberation. According to the *Prashna Upanishad* and many other Eastern scriptures, the aperture through which the soul leaves the body is what indicates the course of its journey after death. In yogic terms, one of the vital airs, the *udana prana*, moves within the main subtle nerve channel and carries the soul to its appropriate exit. The soul of one who has become united with the supreme Consciousness in this life, or who is so completely focused on that direction that he will reach that state after death, passes out through a tiny aperture in the crown of the head known as the *brahmarandhra* or *vidriti*. The *Katha Upanishad* states: "Going upward through that, one becomes immortal." To exit through this aperture has been likened to trying to pass a thread through a very fine needle— if even one fiber of desire is sticking out, the thread can jam. To accomplish this task, one's focus must be attuned by constant practice so that it is totally one-pointed.

The soul of a virtuous person may depart through any of the other apertures in the head: the eyes, nose, or mouth. It then travels along a path of light until it reaches a subtle plane of existence, such as heaven or the realm of ancestors, where it settles to enjoy the fruits of good actions, or karma. But the Hindu and Buddhist scriptures, along with some Egyptian and Greek writings, tell us that these are but temporary realms, where one is welcome to stay until one's good merits are exhausted and the time comes for the soul to be reborn on earth. Those whose actions on earth have been lacking in virtue leave the body through the lower openings and travel a path of darkness to experience the fruits of bad actions until the next cycle begins. These subtle planes of heaven and hell are described in similar terms by practically all traditions.

In the *Brihadaranyaka Upanishad*, the sage Yajnavalkya tells us that when we go to sleep, we take along the material of this world and create a dream state, which is perceived by means of our own "brightness." It is this same light of consciousness, he says, that is present at death:

> When this self gets to weakness, gets to confusedness, as it were, then the breaths gather around him. He takes to himself those particles of light and descends into the heart....The point of his heart becomes lighted up and by that light the self departs either through the eye or through the head or through other apertures of the body.

What happens to the aspirant, the seeker, who has set out on the path of union but has not become one-pointed at the time of death? In the *Bhagavad Gita*, Lord Krishna assures us that "Neither in this life nor the hereafter is there destruction for him, for no one who does good, dear friend, ever treads the path of woe." He tells us that such a seeker will enjoy the fruits of a heavenly plane for a while, then be reborn into a pure and prosperous family, or a family of yogis. There the soul regains the mental impressions that had been developed in its previous life, and with this as a starting point, strives again for perfection.

The importance of choosing a life in which one will meet a master is a point the different traditions agree upon. The *Tibetan Book of the Dead* instructs:

> If one must be reborn on earth, look over the possibilities and choose a good birth; one that will assure continuation of spiritual progress, and that will assure the meeting with a Guru who is a virtuous friend, so that you will thus attain liberation.

In the Indian tradition it is said that aspirants who have faith in and devotion for their master are assured salvation by their master at the time of death. By entering into a state of deep meditation at death, they have an awareness of what is happening and are free of fear.

In Zen, death in a seated or standing position is considered worthy of an enlightened person. Some Zen masters depart this life voluntarily; this is true in other traditions as well. However, it is the dying person's state of mind rather than ability to control the manner of dying that is most important among all three of the traditions we are discussing.

FINAL THOUGHTS, LAST WORDS

The direction that the vital air, *udana prana*, takes is determined by the final thoughts a person has at the time of death. Our last moments of thought create the impetus and circumstances of our rebirth. The final thought, however, cannot simply be the result of a controlled act of will, or a whim. As the twelfth-century Indian poet-saint Jnaneshwar tell us:

> *The longings that a person feels when alive,*
> *Which remain fixed in his heart,*
> *Come to mind at the moment of death.*

The Buddha compared the last moments of thought to a herd of cows in a barn. When the barn door is opened, the strongest will go out first. If no one cow is particularly strong, then the habitual leader will go out first. If no such cow exists, the one nearest the door will go out first. In the absence of any of these, they will all try to get out at once.

Perhaps the last thoughts that are most widely remembered are those of the great being Mahatma Gandhi. When the assassin's bullet hit him, Gandhi immediately invoked the name of his beloved deity with the exclamation, "Sri Ram, Sri Ram, Sri Ram!"

In the *Bhagavad Gita*, Lord Krishna reveals to Arjuna that one may be liberated from rebirth by concentrating completely, by keeping the mind and heart united, by deeply surrendering to the Lord, and by uttering the mantra *Om* while dying. Yet, as the stories in this book suggest, even the first of these tasks is impossible without engaging in some sort of spiritual practice while we are alive.

Often the last words of great masters take the form of blessings, teachings, or instructions. In the Japanese tradition, Buddhist masters and many lay people on the verge of death give their last words in the form of a death poem, or *jisei*. All conven-

16

tional rules of politeness that apply in one's life are broken in these poems—symbolizing the breaking of the constraints of this world. Death poems form the core of Japan's spiritual legacy. In them, the idea of transience is often expressed through images of the changing seasons, with wilting flower petals, for example, as a symbol for death.

In his fascinating book *Japanese Death Poems,* Yoel Hoffmann tells us that while the notion of individual salvation has little place in the Japanese view of death, to the Zen Buddhist the solution to life's enigma is to be found within one's own mind. Hoffmann aptly describes the Zen posture: one must purify one's consciousness and see reality as it is, in its "suchness." And pure reality, as seen through an enlightened mind, does not admit of such polarities as "life" and "death." Enlightenment in the Zen tradition is identified with a state of natural simplicity that extends to one's dying moments.

As we will see in the stories and death poems that follow, many Zen masters leave this world with a casual indifference that we in the West may find difficult to even imagine. Those who follow the "Middle Way" of Buddhism believe that salvation from the world of sorrow and pain is not to be attained by passing from a state of inferior being to a more exalted state, but by ceasing all dualistic thought and resting in this state transcending all duality. One who dies lusting for life in this world or for salvation in the next is not enlightened.

In the Zen tradition, to die is nothing special. In her foreword to Helen Tworkov's *Zen in America,* Natalie Goldberg tells a marvelous story which exemplifies the calm attitude of a great Zen master when facing the imminent prospect of death:

When a rebel army took over a Korean town, all fled the Zen temple except the abbot. The rebel general burst into the temple, and was incensed to find that the master refused to greet him, let alone receive him as a conqueror.

"Don't you know," shouted the general, "that you are looking at one who can run you through without batting an eye?"

"And you," said the abbot, "are looking at one who can be run through without batting an eye!"

The general's scowl turned into a smile. He bowed low and left the temple.

Roughly a dozen death poems are scattered throughout the book for the reader to contemplate and reflect upon; a few additional ones will be found included in the stories.

SPIRITUAL PRACTICE AFTER DEATH

As many hospice workers today can attest, dying does not occur at a precise moment in time: it is not a clear-cut event, but rather a process. In Tibet, the art of leaving the body is known as *phowa*, and death is regarded as a mere point on a continuum marking the transition from one form of consciousness to another. According to the Vajrayana tradition of Tibetan Buddhism, it is important that one continue one's spiritual practice in the period during and immediately after death. Long before death is near, followers of this path study the *Bardo Thodol*, or *Tibetan Book of the Dead* under the tutelage of a master so they can properly navigate the various *bardo*, or stages of death, as each manifests itself. As the dying person's life-force withdraws from the body, a great clear light appears—the light reported in so many near-death experiences. The Tibetan masters teach that if one can recognize and merge into it, one is liberated from all separate existence. However, as mentioned earlier while discussing the Hindu tradition, only one who has developed total one-pointedness will be able to take advantage of this crucial moment. If the moment is lost, one continues on the journey through the after-death world, and is presented with other opportunities to move toward liberation, or at least a good birth.

The *Tibetan Book of the Dead* charts the basic experiences one has at the time of death and points out the signposts leading to different realms. At death, as in dreams, we inhabit a world composed of mental images. It is critical to understand that these realms are creations of the mind. One whose spirit has acquired the agility of dispassion is able to recognize various experiences in the death state as aspects of his or her own consciousness, and thus is able to navigate gracefully through the different situations as they manifest.

In his contemporary masterpiece, *The Tibetan Book of Living and Dying*, Sogyal Rinpoche tells us that at the moment of death "the ordinary mind and its delusions die, and in that gap the boundless sky-like nature of our mind is uncovered. This essential nature of mind is the background to the whole of life and death, like the sky, which folds the whole universe in its embrace." As we see in some of the stories that follow, deaths of Tibetan masters are often accompanied by miraculous signs and portentous omens, such as rainbows, divine music or fragrance, flowers showering down from the sky, and earthquakes.

In the Indian tradition of Yoga, as karmic impressions are burned in the inner "fire" kindled by the guru, eventually a moment comes when one experiences one's own death while in a meditative state. In *Does Death Really Exist?* Swami Muktananda writes:

> Once one has had that experience, one is never again afraid of death. Therefore, when the moment comes to die in meditation, one should die completely. Then one will come back to life in such a way that one will never die again.

In such a spiritual death—dying to the ego while still alive—fear of physical dying is overcome and one becomes saturated with an awareness of the "eternal spirit" that Hindus call *moksha*. In *Meditation and the Art of Dying*, Pandit Arya tells us that in the Hindu tradition a guru sometimes transmits to a very rare disciple a *diksha-mytyu*, or initiatory death experience:

> This initiatory death is a conscious process in yoga whereby a hale and hearty person may experience death for a little while. Not everyone can withstand it. But those few who are given that kind of initiation…are never the same again. The meaning of life and death completely changes for them.

This quote immediately calls to mind the thousands of near-death experiences that have been chronicled by researchers such as Dr. Raymond Moody. Of the many spiritual groups in India that practice anticipatory dying, perhaps the most well known are the Bauls of Bengal. Poets and mystics, the Bauls were ecstatic *bhaktas* (devotees of Vishnu or Krishna) who practiced meditating on their own death in order to surrender themselves to and be reborn in God—dead to the personal self yet fully alive.

Buddhism also teaches that the best way to prepare for one's own death is to anticipate the death experience while alive. The Buddha urged his disciples to meditate on this sacred mystery. According to the *Mahaparinirvana Sutra*, as he was approaching his own death, the Buddha said:

> *Of all footprints*
> *That of the elephant is supreme;*
> *Of all mindfulness meditations*
> *That on death is supreme.*

Thus, when the seventeenth-century Zen master Suzuki Shosan was told that his illness was a grave one, he responded that it meant nothing, since he had already died (presumably in meditation) more than thirty years before.

WHAT HAPPENS TO A MASTER'S SOUL AFTER DEATH?

Seppo said to Gensha, "Monk Shinso asked me where a certain dead monk has gone, and I told him it was like ice becoming water." Gensha said, "That was all right, but I myself would not have answered like that." "What would you have said?" asked Seppo. Gensha replied, "It's like water returning to water."

In her book *Being Nobody, Going Nowhere*, Ayya Khema presents us with another delightful response to this question:

> Once the Buddha was asked by the wanderer Vacchagotta, "Sir, what happens to the Enlightened One

after death? Where does he go?" The Buddha said, "Wanderer, make a fire from the sticks that are lying around here." So he did and he lit the fire. Then the Buddha said, "Now throw some more sticks on to it." He did, and the Buddha asked, "What's happening?" Vacchagotta answered, "Oh, the fire's going well." The Buddha said, "Now stop throwing sticks on it." And after a while the fire went out. The Buddha said to him, "What happened to the fire?" "The fire's gone out, Sir." The Buddha said, "Well, where did it go? Did it go forward? Backward? Right? Left? Up or down?" The wanderer said, "No it didn't. It just went out." The Buddha said, "That's right. That's exactly what happens to the Enlightened One after death."

When no more sticks are thrown on the fire of passionate desire, of craving, of wanting, then the fire goes out. Since there is no karma being created by such a master, there is nothing that needs to be reborn.

The spiritual masters portrayed in this book are of many different persuasions. Among the Indian masters, some are *bhaktas*, or lovers of God; some are *jnanis*, devoted to wisdom; some are *karma yogis*, who achieved their state through selfless service; and some were born self-perfected masters. In the Zen Buddhist tradition of China and Japan, masters from both the Rinzai sect, the path that supports instant realization, and the Soto sect, the path of gradual realization, are represented. Within the Tibetan tradition, some masters are well-known lamas and *rinpoches*, while others are seemingly ordinary people whose elevated state was recognized by others only during their final dying moments.

As is invariably the case with hagiographies, these stories have been told and retold, some of them for centuries. While a few stories have the quality of legend about them, my interest has been in presenting actual death experiences. The list of masters presented here is not meant to be comprehensive, but rather to show a cross-section from these three traditions. A few death stories of masters from the Taoist, Muslim, and earlier Buddhist traditions have also found their way irresistibly into the text. A selection of death stories from the Judeo-Christian and other traditions not represented here might make a fascinating sequel to this book.

As you read through these stories, you may want to savor the feelings or attitudes these great masters embody as they are dying. Sit and contemplate one of the underlying qualities—such as joy, courage, fearlessness, humility, or simplicity—and reflect on how you can acquire that quality in your own life. Another fruitful practice is to hold the reality of your own death in front of you each day. This often throws everything into a clearer and sharper perspective, and our priorities naturally rearrange themselves, yielding a richer and more deeply satisfying time spent on this planet.

All the great masters wish for us one thing: that we become able to identify with the true part of our being—our essence, our inner self, our soul—before we leave our physical body. Death is natural and unavoidable. But, from the viewpoint of Eastern mystics, it is not real. Only union with the Absolute, immersion in the Void, is real. In compiling these stories, I have entered more deeply into my understanding of death and erased many fears associated with it. I hope that you, the reader, have a similar experience.

This book is written for those who are on, or who aspire to be on, the spiritual path. It is written for seekers. This term, as I use it, is very broad. It includes all those who consider the unseen in life to be their true source of nourishment, sustenance, and joy.

EDITOR'S NOTE

For those unfamiliar with the three traditions represented here, foreign terms are usually rendered in italics and given translations. Exceptions to this are words such as guru, lama, ashram, and nirvana, which have come into wide use in English, as well as two Sanskrit terms that appear with frequency in this book and may require explanation: *dharma* and *samadhi*.

In both Hinduism and Buddhism *dharma* is a central concept. In the sense that it is used here, it means "the teachings," the fundamental understanding of the nature of reality embodied in these religious traditions. *Samadhi* originally referred to a deep meditative state in which the duality of subject and object disappears. In the Buddhist tradition this sense of the word has largely been retained. But in the Hindu or Yogic traditions, *samadhi* also came to mean a realized master's departure from this life (the word *mahasamadhi*, or "great *samadhi*" is also used in this sense), and by extension, it even became the term for the tomb or mausoleum of a great teacher. The context should make clear to the reader which sense is meant.

Rendering of Asian names is problematic because of the many systems of romanization in use; this book follows the various conventions employed in the original sources.

GRACEFUL
EXITS

1

When an elder Buddhist master asked a group of meditators, "What survives when an enlightened being dies?" a man in the group replied, "When an enlightened being dies, nothing remains."

The Master smiled and replied to the surprise of those assembled: "No. The truth remains."

2

When it became clear that he was about to die, Matsuo Basho, the greatest of the haiku poets, was asked by his friends for a death poem, but he refused them. He claimed that in a sense every poem he had written in the previous decade—by far his most productive period, and one of deep Zen involvement—had been done as if a death poem. Yet the next morning, the poet called his friends to his bedside and told them that during the night he had dreamed, and that on waking a poem had come to him. He then recited this famous poem:

Sick, on a journey,
Yet over withered fields
Dreams wander on.

Senior disciples assembled at his bedside as Zen Master Taji approached death. One of them, remembering the master was fond of a certain kind of cake, had spent half a day searching the pastry shops of Tokyo for this confection, which he now presented to him. With a wan smile the dying master accepted a piece of the cake and slowly began munching it. As he grew weaker, his disciples inquired whether he had any final words for them.

"Yes," the master replied.

The disciples leaned forward eagerly so as not to miss a word. "Please tell us!"

"My, but this cake is delicious!"

And with that he slipped away.

Neem Karoli Baba, also known as Maharaji, spent what was to be his final day at his ashram at Kainchi immersed in meeting his devotees, chanting, and prayer. Twice he put one of his Indian devotees into *samadhi* and brought him out of it by throwing his blanket over the man's head. At one point he said to those gathered, "He is your guru. He is young and I am old. He will live and I will die!"

Maharaji hinted that he was leaving for several days and later announced: "Today, I am released from Central Jail forever." Accompanied by two devotees, Maharaji set off for a day trip to Agra to visit a heart specialist because of chest pains he had been having. Following the visit, the specialist said his heart was fine

Neem Karoli Baba

and he just needed rest. At 9:00 PM he left for the train station to return home.

Shortly after departing Agra, Maharaji and two of his devotees got off the train at Mathura. Maharaji was sitting on the steps of the station when he began convulsing. His eyes were closed and his body was cold and sweating. Maharaji asked to be taken to nearby Vrindaban; during the taxi ride there, he seemed unconscious, though he would occasionally mumble incomprehensibly. His devotees took him to the emergency room, where he was given injections and an oxygen mask. The hospital staff said that he was in a diabetic coma but that his pulse was fine. When Maharaji came to, he pulled off the oxygen mask and the blood pressure band, saying, *"Bekar* [useless]." Maharaji asked for Ganga water, but as there was none, he was given regular water. He then repeated *"Jaya Jagadish Hare* [Hail to the Lord of the Universe]" several times, each time in a lower pitch. His face became very peaceful; all signs of pain disappeared. He was dead.

After his death, Maharaji's body was brought from Vrindaban to the veranda of the ashram in Kainchi and placed on a large block of ice. In the evening it was paraded through the streets atop a car. Thousands watched the procession, which was complete with brass band and processional lights. At about 9:00 PM, Maharaji's body was placed on the funeral pyre in the courtyard of the temple.

⤶ 5 ⤷

When Zen Master Takuan Soho was dying, his disciples asked him to write a death verse. He demurred at first, saying, "I have no last words." They pleaded with him, so he took up a brush, wrote the character for "dream," and passed away.

When death finally comes you will welcome it like an
old friend, being aware of how dreamlike
and impermanent the phenomenal world really is.
—Dilgo Khyentse Rinpoche

⤳ 6 ⤳

Although Anandamayi Ma traveled to many parts of India, the Kankhal ashram was to become her final resting place. In July of 1982, her health began to deteriorate seriously. As she weakened day by day, her devotees encouraged her to eat and drink, but she resisted. They implored her to perform a manifestation of spontaneous divine will, *kheyala*, on her body. However, she repeatedly responded, "There is no *kheyala*. Whatever God does is all right." Toward the end of July, she instructed devotees to take her to the Kishenpur ashram in Dehradun. She was to stay in her second floor room there, amidst the sounds of uninterrupted chanting and prayers in the hall below, until she breathed her last breath on August 27. In accord with a wish she had made before her death to go to Kanghal, her body was taken on a twenty-seven-mile procession to the Kanghal ashram. Although Ma had never taken the formal *sannyasini* vows, she was buried according to strict scriptural injunctions.

Anandamayi Ma

Her shrine today remains a place of pilgrimage renowned for its spiritual power.

⌒ 7 ⌒

Hakuin Ekaku, revered as one of the greatest teachers and artists in the history of Japanese Zen, lived in semiretirement for the last three years of his life. In the winter of 1768, he was examined by a doctor, who, as he felt Hakuin's pulse, remarked, "Everything seems all right." Hakuin grumbled back, "Some doctor. He can't see that in three days I'll be gone."

At dawn on December 11, Hakuin awoke from a peaceful sleep, let loose a terrific shout, rolled over on his right side, and died. After his cremation, Hakuin's ashes were said to be the lustrous color of coral and as fragrant as spice.

His final piece of calligraphy was his life statement: a giant character for "midst," with the inscription, "Meditation in the MIDST of action is a billion times superior to meditation in stillness."

⌒ 8 ⌒

Lama Tseten, disciple of the modern Tibetan master Jamyang Khyentse Rinpoche and tutor to the master's spiritual wife Khandro Tsering Chodron, died in an extraordinary way. Although there was a monastery close by, he refused to go there, saying he did not want to leave a corpse for them to clear up. Khandro was nursing and caring for her old tutor; suddenly one evening he called her over to his side. He had an endearing way

33

of calling her "A-mi," meaning "my child" in his local dialect. "A-mi," he said tenderly, "come here. It's happening now. I've no further advice for you. You are fine as you are: I am happy with you. Serve your master just as you have been doing."

Immediately she turned to run out of the tent, but he caught her by the sleeve. "Where are you gong?" he asked. "I'm going to call Rinpoche," she replied.

"Don't bother him, there's no need," he smiled. "With the the master, there's no such thing as distance." With that, he just gazed up into the sky and passed away.

Khandro ran to fetch Jamyang Khyentse. As he entered the tent, he gave one look at Lama Tseten's face, and then, peering into his eyes, began to chuckle. He always used to call him La Gen ["old Lama"], a sign of his affection. "La Gen," he said, "don't stay in that state!" He could see that Lama Tseten was doing a particular meditation practice in which the practitioner merges the nature of his mind with the space of truth. "You know, La Gen, when you do this practice, sometimes subtle obstacles can arise. Come on, I'll guide you."

Transfixed, those present watched what happened next with disbelief. Lama Tseten came back to life. Jamyang Kyhentse stayed by his side and took him through the *phowa*, the practice for guiding one's consciousness at the moment before death. There are many ways of doing this practice; the one he used then culminated with the master uttering the syllable "A" three times. As the he declared the first "A," Lama Tseten was heard accompanying him quite audibly. The second time his voice was less distinct, and the third time it was silent; he had gone.

Lama Tseten's death was a display of spiritual mastery.

Empty-handed I entered the world
Barefoot I leave it.
My coming, my going—
Two simple happenings
That got entangled.

—Kozan Ichigyo
fourteenth-century Zen monk

Death is not our shadow, it is our guide.

—Gurumayi Chidvilasananda

⤛ 9 ⤜

A devotee named Cholappa had an earnest desire for the mortal remains of his master, Akkalkot Swami, to be enshrined at his home. To this end, Cholappa dug a place in the compound of his house and built a *samadhi*, or relic chamber. One day, while passing by Cholappa's house, the all-knowing swami said, "Cholappa, I shall put you in that ditch first; I shall not be leaving before you pack off!" A few months later, Cholappa died of cholera.

In his later years, Akkalkot Swami reclined in bed, covered with a cloth blanket. Thousands of devotees and seekers would visit him each day for *darshan* [audience with, or even a glimpse of, a spiritual master]. One day the swami developed a high temperature that did not subside, and stopped taking food. When one of his devotees asked his permission to take him in a palanquin to his favorite place—the banyan tree—he agreed. To a devotee who asked, "Swamiji, when are you going to recover?" he replied, "There is no question of my recovery. The time has come for me to depart." Doctors rushed to him with medicines, but he never took them. When the devotee repeated the question, he replied: "When mountains beckon to me." To another devotee who asked the same question, he responded, "When Pandharpur is on fire." [Some present thought this to mean whenever the teachings and righteousness are in peril.]

Then Akkalkot Swami sent for his favorite barber and had a clean shave and bath. Although he hadn't taken food in a week, he looked quite cheerful. He greeted each of those around him with a solicitous look and inquired as to their welfare. Then, seated in the lotus position, he spoke his last words: "No one should weep—I shall be always present at all places. I shall respond to every call of the devotees." With these words his eyes closed. The peace and radiance on his face increased, and three white sparks flashed from his mouth. Devotees thronged to the banyan tree and a mammoth procession assembled and went around the city in regal splendor. After the body was appropriately worshiped, it was placed inside the *samadhi* at Cholappa's house.

ꝏ 10 ꝏ

As Master Tenno was dying, he called to his room the monk in charge of food and clothing in the temple. When the monk sat down by the bed, Master Tenno asked, "Do you understand?"

"No," the monk replied.

Tenno, picking up his pillow, hurled it through the window, and fell back dead.

ꝏ 11 ꝏ

It is recorded that three months prior to the Buddha's death the earth was afflicted by a mighty earthquake and a storm. His disciple Ananda inquired of him as to the meaning of these omens, whereupon he replied, "This earthquake portends that I have sacrificed the remaining years of my life. Reckoned from today,

I will sustain my life for only three more months." Three months later, as Buddha and his disciples came to a mango grove, they were approached by a householder called Chunda, who invited them to a meal. Buddha accepted, but later instructed his disciples that he alone was to eat of the food to be offered. After the meal, he became ill, and insisted that they walk on to Kushinagar. There he bathed and then asked Ananda to make him a bed. "O Ananda," he said to his grief-stricken disciple, "the time has come for me to pass into peace. Go and tell the others about it, for they will be upset should they not witness my passing."

When all had gathered, the Buddha gave them a final sermon.

> It is not appropriate to grieve in an hour of joy... You all weep, but is there any cause for grief? We should look upon a sage as a person escaped from a burning mansion... It does not matter whether I am here or not; salvation does not depend upon me but upon practicing the Dharma, just as a cure depends not upon seeing the doctor but upon taking his medicine... My time has come, my work is done... Everything eventually comes to an end, even if it should last for an eon. The time of parting is bound to one day come. I have done what I could for myself and others, and to remain longer would be without purpose. I have trained all whom I could train. My teachings shall last for many generations, so do not be disturbed. Recognize that all that lives is subject to the laws of impermanence, and strive for eternal wisdom. When the light of knowledge dispels ignorance, when the world is seen as without substance, the end of life is seen as peace and as a cure to a disease. Everything that

exists is bound to perish. Be therefore mindful of your
salvation. The time of my passing has come.

With these words the Buddha entered into a profound meditation
and passed away. The earth shook like a ship in a storm, and
thunder and lightning filled the heavens.

⌒ 1 2 ⌒

After taking leave of his teacher Huang-po, Lin-chi—often called
the Chinese Socrates—went on a long pilgrimage before settling
in a small temple around 850. He taught there about ten years
and then retired. In 866, when he was about to die, he seated
himself and said, "After I am extinguished, do not let my True
Dharma Eye be extinguished." A monk came forward and said,
"How could I let your True Dharma Eye be extinguished?" Lin-
chi asked, "When somebody asks you about it, what will you say
to him?" The monk gave a shout. "Who would have thought my
True Dharma Eye would be extinguished upon reaching this
blind ass!" said Lin-chi. Then the master, although not ill, adjust-
ed his robes, sat erect, and died.

⌒ 1 3 ⌒

Kalu Rinpoche tried to sit up by himself but had difficulty doing
so. Lama Gyaltsen, feeling that this was perhaps the time, sup-
ported Rinpoche's back as he sat up, and Bokar Tulku Rinpoche
took his extended hand. Kalu Rinpoche wanted to sit absolutely
straight, but the attending doctor and nurse were upset by this, so
he relaxed his posture slightly. Nevertheless, he assumed the

Kalu Rinpoche

meditation posture—his eyes gazed outward in meditation gaze, and his lips moved softly. A profound feeling of peace and happiness settled on the room and spread through the minds of those present. Slowly Kalu Rinpoche's gaze and his eyelids lowered, and the breath stopped.

Before we know it our life is finished and it is time to die.
If we lack the foundation of a stable practice,
we go to death helplessly, in fear and anguish.

—Kalu Rinpoche

⌒ 14 ⌒

As Chuang-tzu approached death, his disciples wanted to give him a large and expensive funeral. But Chuang-tzu said, "The heavens and the earth will serve me as a coffin and a coffin shell. The sun and moon and stars will decorate my bier. All creation will be at hand to witness the event. What more need I than these?"

His disciples gasped, "We're afraid that carrion kites and crows will eat the body of our master!"

Chuang-tzu replied, "Above the ground my flesh will feed the crows and kites; below the ground, the ants and cricket-moles. Why rob one to feed the other?" And then he smiled. "I shall have Heaven and Earth for my coffin," he said. "The sun and moon will be the jade symbols hanging by my side. All the planets and constellations will shine as jewels around me. All beings will be present as mourners at the wake. What more could I need? Everything has been taken care of."

⇐ 15 ⇒

Sensing that death was near, Master Razan called everyone into the Buddha Hall and ascended the lecture seat. First he held his left hand open for several minutes. No one understood, so he told the monks from the eastern side of the monastery to leave. Then he held his right hand open. Still no one understood, so he told the monks from the western side of the monastery to leave. Only the laymen remained. He said to them: "If any of you really want to show gratitude to Buddha for his compassion to you, spare no efforts in spreading the Dharma. Now, get out! Get out of here!" Then, laughing loudly, the master fell over dead.

⇐ 16 ⇒

In 1885, Ramakrishna developed cancer of the throat, and steadily grew worse. On August 15 of the following year, realizing that his end was near, Ramakrishna assured his wife, Sarada Devi, that she would be all right and that his young disciples would take care of her as they had of him. He died the next day. In his last days, he addressed himself saying, "O mind, do not worry about the body. Let the body and its pain take care of each other. Think of the Holy Mother [Sarada Devi] and be happy."

After the cremation of his body, Sarada was removing her jewelry, as Hindu widows do, when Ramakrishna appeared to

42

Ramakrishna

her. In the vision, he told her not to remove her jewelry, assuring her that he had not gone away but had only passed from one room to another. Confident of his continual presence with her, the Holy Mother, as she was known to her devotees, committed herself to teaching and guiding the young disciples who had been left in her care.

The body and the soul!
The body was born and it will die.
But for the soul there is no death.
It is like the betel nut. When the nut is ripe it does not
stick to the shell. But when it is green it is difficult to
separate from the shell. After realizing God, one does not
identify anymore with the body. Then one knows the body
and the soul are two different things.
—Ramakrishna

 17

Five days before her own death thirty-four years later, Sarada Devi made a significant utterance while consoling a visiting devotee who had sobbed out, "Mother, what will happen to us hereafter?" In a very low voice, promptly came the reassuring words, "Why do you fear? You have seen the Master." Then after a pause, she solemnly added, "But I tell you one thing—if you want peace of mind, do not find fault with others. Rather see your own faults. Learn to make the whole world your own. No one is a stranger, my child; this entire world is your own!"

On the eve of her departure, the Mother said, "Sharat, I am going. Yogen, Gopap and the rest are here. You look after them." On July 20, 1920 at 1:30 AM, the Holy Mother, in a final ecstasy, left the physical world.

⌒ 18 ⌒

Before he died, Hui-neng, the sixth Chinese patriarch of Zen, spoke these moving words of farewell:

> Come close. In the eighth month I intend to leave this world. If any of you have doubts, ask about them quickly, and I shall resolve them for you. I must bring your delusions to an end and make it possible for you to gain peace. After I have gone there will be no one to teach you.

Deeply touched, all the disciples began to cry. Among them Shen-hui alone remained unmoved. Hui-neng turned and spoke to him:

> Shen-hui, you are a young monk, yet you have attained the [status of awakening] in which good and not good are identical, and you are not moved by judgments of praise and blame. You others have not yet understood... You're crying just because you don't know where I'm going. If you knew where I was going you wouldn't be crying. Nature itself is without birth and without destruction, without going and without coming.

Hui-neng's last words were these:

Good-bye, all of you. I shall depart from you now. After I am gone, do not weep worldly tears, nor accept condolences, money, and silks from people, nor wear mourning garments. If you did so it would not accord with the sacred Dharma, nor would you be true disciples of mine. Be the same as you would if I were here, and sit all together in meditation. If you are only peacefully calm and quiet, without motion, without stillness, without birth, without destruction, without coming, without going, without judgments of right and wrong, without staying and without going—this then is the Great Way. After I have gone just practice according to the Dharma in the same way that you did on the days that I was with you. Even though I were still to be in this world, if you went against the teachings, there would be no use in my having stayed here.

⌒ 19 ⌒

According to the Dzogchen teachings of the Nyingmapa school of Tibetan Buddhism, advanced practitioners can end their lives in a remarkable way, causing their bodies to be reabsorbed back into the light essence of the elements that created them; a manner of passing that is called the "rainbow body."

In 1952 there was a famous instance of the rainbow body in the east of Tibet, witnessed by many people. The man who attained it, Sonam Namgyal, was a humble person, an itinerant stonecarver of mantras and sacred texts. Some say he had been a hunter in his youth, and had received teaching from a great master. No one really knew he was a practitioner; he was truly what is called a "hidden yogin." Some time before his death, he would go up into the mountains and just sit, silhouetted against the sky-line, gazing up into space. He composed his own songs and chants and sang them instead of the traditional ones. No one had any idea what he was doing. He fell ill, but, strange to say, became increasingly happy. When the illness got worse, his family called in masters and doctors. His son told him he should remember all the teachings he had heard, and he smiled and said, "I've forgotten them all and anyway, there's nothing to remember. Everything is illusion, but I am confident that all is well."

Just before his death at seventy-nine, he said: "All I ask is that when I die, don't move my body for a week." When he died his family wrapped his body and invited lamas and monks to come and practice for him. They placed the body in a small room in the house, and they could not help noticing that though he had been a tall person, they had no trouble getting it in, as if he were becoming smaller. At the same time, an extra-ordinary display of rainbow-colored light was seen all around the house. When they looked into the room on the sixth day, they saw that the body was getting smaller and smaller. On the eighth day after his death, the morning on which the funeral had been arranged, the undertakers arrived to collect his body. When they undid its coverings, they found nothing inside but his nails and hair.

≈ 20 ≈

Having called his monks together, Master Hofuku announced: "During the last week my energy has been draining—certainly no cause for worry. It's just that death is near."

A monk asked, "You are about to die. What meaning does it have? We will continue living. What meaning does that have?"

"They are both the Way," the Master replied.

"But how can I reconcile the two?" asked the monk.

Hofuku answered, "When it rains it pours," and wrapping his legs in the full lotus, calmly died.

⌒ 2 1 ⌒

Sai Baba of Shirdi, the famous Indian saint, was revered by Hindus and Muslims alike. What follows is a description of a deep trance state known as the "seventy-two hour *samadhi,*" that Sai Baba experienced in 1886, and an account of his *mahasamadhi,* or final liberation from his physical body, some thirty years later.

One full moon day in 1886, Sai Baba suffered from a severe attack of asthma. To rid himself of it, he decided to elevate his *prana,* or life force, and go into *samadhi.* He told one of his disciples: "Protect my body for three days. If I return it will be all right; if I do not, bury my body in that open land (pointing to it) and fix two flags there as a mark." Having said this, at about 10:00 PM Baba fell to the ground. Both his breathing and his pulse stopped. It seemed as if his *prana* had left the body. The villagers came, wanting to hold an inquest and bury the body in the place Baba had designated. But one of his disciples, Mhalsapati, prevented them from doing so. He remained seated, with his Master's body on his lap, for the full three days. Finally, at 3:00 AM on the third day Baba showed signs of life—his abdomen began to move as his breathing began again. Opening his eyes and stretching his limbs, Baba returned to consciousness.

Two years before his death in 1918, Sai Baba confided to two of his disciples that a third disciple, Tatya, would die during the time of the festival Dasara, two years hence. He made them vow not to reveal this information to anyone. The years passed and Tatya fell sick at the time Baba indicated, but unexpectedly Sai Baba also developed a fever. As Dasara approached, the two devotees were quite concerned about their friend Tatya, for he grew steadily worse. As the main day of Dasara dawned, Tatya's pulse became weak. His end was apparently at hand. But the two disciples were entirely unprepared for what was actually to transpire: by noon Tatya began to show signs of improvement, but at 2:30 PM Sai Baba left his body! In recording this strange event, Nagesh Gunaji, Sai Baba's biographer, says: "People said that Baba gave up his life for Tatya. Why did he do so? He alone knows, as his ways are inscrutable. It seems, however, that in this incident, Baba gave a hint of his passing away, substituting Tatya's name for his own."

Anticipating his departure, Sai Baba sent word to another saint that "the light that Allah lit, he is taking away." The saint received the message with tears.

Shortly before his death, echoing somewhat the words of Sri Krishna to his disciple, Arjuna, Sai Baba said to his own disciples:

> He who loves me most, always sees me. The whole world is desolate without me. He tells no stories but mine. He ceaselessly meditates upon me and always chants my name. I feel indebted to him who surrenders himself completely to me and ever remembers me. I shall repay this debt by giving him salvation [self-realization]. I am dependent upon him who thinks and hungers after me

Coming, all is clear,
no doubt about it.
Going, all is clear,
without a doubt.
What, then, is it all?

—Hosshin
thirteenth-century Zen monk

and who does not eat anything without first offering it to me. He who thus comes to me, becomes one with me, just as a river goes to the sea and becomes one with it. So, leaving pride and egoism, you should surrender yourself to me who am seated in your heart.

Although Sai Baba attained *mahasamadhi* in 1918, he promised: "I shall remain active and vigorous even after leaving this earthly body. I am ever living to help those who come to me and who surrender and seek refuge in me." At another time, he said: "My shrine will bless my devotees and fulfill their needs. My relics will speak from the tomb."

⎝ 2 2 ⎜

Sai Baba, when still a boy, had been present at the death of his own master, Venkusha (also known as Gopal Rao). One day, as the lad was in attendance on the master, some other young boys threw bricks at him, out of jealousy. The first missed, but when a second brick was flung, Venkusha took the blow, and his head began to bleed profusely. The young Sai Baba was moved to tears and begged his master to send him away so that the master would not be harmed because of proximity to him. Venkusha refused, but after bandaging his injury he suddenly said, "I see that the time has come to part from you. Tomorrow at 4:00 PM I shall leave this body, not as a result of this injury, but by my own power... Therefore, I shall now invest my full spiritual personality in you." He proceeded to give the lad a special type of initiation called *diksha*. At the appointed time on the following day, in a state of perfect peace, Venkusha left his body.

Just before Master Bassui passed away, at the age of sixty-one, he sat up in the lotus posture and said to the disciples gathered around him, "Look directly! What is this? Look in this manner and you won't be fooled." He repeated this injunction in a loud voice, then calmly died.

At his own request, he was buried under a shrine he had built to honor Kannon, bodhisattva of compassion. According to Bassui, Kannon was "a person who for every sound he heard contemplated the mind of the hearer, realizing his own nature"— the core of Bassui's own life and teachings.

I know you are very ill. Like a good Zen student, you are facing that sickness squarely. You may not know exactly who is suffering, but question yourself: What is the essence of this mind? Think only of this. You will need no more. Covet nothing. Your end, which is endless, is as a snowflake dissolving in the pure air.

—Bassui, addressing a dying disciple

Almost blind at the age of ninety-six and no longer able to teach or work about the monastery, Yamamoto Gempo Roshi decided it was time to die, so he stopped eating. When asked by his monks why he refused his food, he replied that he had outlived his use-fulness and was only a bother to everybody. They told him, "If you die now [January] when it is so cold, everyone will be uncomfortable at your funeral and you will be an even greater nuisance, so please eat!" He thereupon resumed eating, but when it grew warm again he stopped, and died quietly not long after.

~ 25 ~

At the age of eighty-two, in the year 1958, Nyogen Senzaki died in America. Instead of writing the traditional Japanese death poem, Nyogen had taped his last words. Mourners were some-what startled when, as they were in the mortuary in the pres-ence of the master's body, surrounded by flowers and the chant-ing of twelve monks, a loud and clear tape recording of Senzaki's voice began to play:

> Friends in the Dharma, be satisfied with your own head. Do not put any false heads above your own. Then minute after minute, watch your steps closely. Always keep your head cold and your feet warm. These are my last words to you... The funeral must be performed in the simplest way. A few friends who live nearby may attend it quietly. Those who know how to recite sutras may murmur the shortest one. That will be enough. Do not ask a priest or anyone to make a long service and speech and have others yawn... Remember me as a monk, and nothing else. I do not belong to any sect or cathedral. None of them should send me a promoted priest's rank or anything of that sort. I like to be free from such trash and die happily.

Part of Nyogen Senzaki's ashes were sent to Soen Roshi and the rest were buried according to his instructions "in some unknown, uncultivated field." He had told his disciples:

> Do not erect a tombstone! The California poppy is tombstone enough... I would like to be like the mushroom in the deep mountains—no flowers, no branches, and no root. I wish to rot most inconspicuously.

☞ 26 ☜

In 1947 Ramana Maharshi's health began to fail. When the doctors suggested amputating his arm above a cancerous tumor, Ramana replied with a smile:

> There is no need for alarm. The body is itself a disease. Let it have its natural end. Why mutilate it? A simple dressing on the affected part will do.

Two more operations had to be performed, but the tumor appeared again. Indigenous systems of medicine were tried, and homeopathy too, but the disease did not yield to treatment. The sage, supremely indifferent to suffering, was quite unconcerned. He sat as a spectator watching the disease waste the body; his eyes shone as bright as ever, and his grace flowed toward all beings. Ramana insisted that the crowds who came in large numbers should be allowed to have his *darshan* [sight of a holy being]. The devotees profoundly wished that the sage would cure his body by using the supernormal powers. Ramana had compassion for those who grieved over the suffering, and he sought to comfort them by reminding them of the truth that Bhagavan was not the body:

54

Ramana Maharshi

They take this body for Bhagavan and attribute suffering to him. What a pity! They are despondent that Bhagavan is going to leave them and go away, but where can he go and how?

The end came on April 14, 1950. That evening the sage gave *darshan* to all the devotees in the ashram. They sat singing Ramana's hymn to Arunacala, the name of the holy mountain the sage so loved. He asked his attendants to help him sit up, and opened his luminous and gracious eyes for a brief while. There was a smile, a tear of bliss trickled down from the outer corner of one of his eyes, and at 8:47 PM his breathing stopped. There was no struggle, no spasm, none of the signs of death. At that very moment, a comet moved slowly across the sky, passed over the summit of the holy hill, Arunacala, and disappeared behind it.

Soul, mind, and ego are mere words. There are no true
entities of the kind. Consciousness is the only truth.
Forgetfulness of your real nature is the real death;
remembrance of it is the true birth.
It puts an end to successive births.

—Ramana Maharshi

☞ 27 ☜

When the poet-saint Kabir fell ill, he refused to have himself treated. Bidding farewell to his physician, he said: "Depart to thy

house, O physician, my malady is beyond thee. He who has created this pain, He will look to my well-being."

After his death in 1518 at Maghar, India (near Gorakhpur)
both Hindus and Muslims fought for his corpse. One group wanted to burn the body and the other wanted to bury it. At last Kabir
himself appeared before them in person: he asked them to lift the
shroud and look beneath it. In the place of the corpse, to their
great astonishment, they found a heap of flowers. One half of the
flowers were taken and buried by the Muslims of Gorakhpur, and
the other half were taken by the Hindus to Benares and burned.

⌒ 28 ⌒

Master Yakusan's manner of death was in keeping with his life.
When he was about to die, he yelled out, "The Dharma Hall is
falling down! The Dharma Hall is falling down!" The monks
brought various things and began to prop it up. The master
clapped his hands and laughed loudly. Then Yakusan threw up
his hands and cried out, "You don't understand my meaning,"
and thereupon passed away.

⌒ 29 ⌒

When his health began to falter, Swami Ram Tirth retired to
some remote ashrams along the Ganges. Dedicating his remaining energies to the study of the Vedas, he would sit cross-legged
in contemplation for days on end, unconcerned about his body.
When Puranji, one of his disciples, noted the absence of his characteristic laughter and vitality, he replied:

Thirty years and more
I worked to nullify myself.
Now I leap the leap of death.
The ground churns up
The skies spin round.

—Rankei Doryu
thirteenth-century Zen monk

Puranji, the world is concerned only with my blossoms—
they taste me when I appear before them in my flowers.
But they do not know how much I have to labor under-
ground in the dark recesses, in my roots, to gather food
for the flowers and the fruits. I am now in my roots.
Silence is greater work than the fireworks of preaching
and giving off thoughts to the world.

Before leaving this world, Ram Tirth's parting words to his disciple Puranji were: "Puranji! Wherever you go, live in the Golden
Land, in the inner light. Carry on the work that Ram has begun,
for the time has come for Ram to take the vow of silence." His
parting words to his disciple Narayana were:

My son, Ram shall soon be silent. His pen and tongue
will fail him. Ram's body is growing weaker day by day;
his mind has gotten so tired of the world that nothing
interests him now. He feels as if he will no more go
down to the plains. No wonder if Ram's body soon
becomes inactive. Never shall he leave his dear Ganga's
bosom. Therefore go to your cave; practice seclusion,
dive deep every moment into Ram and come out as the
embodiment of Vedanta. Have no griefs, no worries, no
sorrows. Feel Ram with you, within you. He is your
body. He is your mind. He is your all in all. He is your
own self. Emerge from your seclusion and be as Ram
himself.

One week later on the holiday known as Diwali, October 12,
1906, Swami Ram Tirth left his body while bathing in the Ganges.
While he was being carried downstream by the current, his cook
heard him say aloud, "Go! Remember thy Mother! If thou art
destined to go thus, go!...Om! Om! Om!" He drew his limbs into

the lotus posture and floated downstream to where the current drew him into an underwater cave.

Only an hour before his death, the cook had noticed the swami writing the following passage with tears of joy dropping from his eyes.

> O death, go and strike my body: I have millions of bodies to live in. I will dress myself in the moonbeams, in the gauze made of fine silvery threads, and pass my time in tranquil rest. I will sing my songs in the form of hill streams and brooks, in the form of the rolling waves; I will move on. I am the soft-footed wind which walks on in ecstasy. I am the ever-gliding form which goes on as time. I descended as waterfalls on the mountain slopes, reviving the faded plants. I made the roses burst into laughter. I made the nightingale sing her mournful ditties; I knocked at the doors and woke up the sleeping ones, wiping the tears of the one, blowing the veil from the face of the other. I teased those near and also far. I teased you too. Lo, I go, I go, with nothing in my possession…

Swami Ram Tirth found the truth he sought by realizing that he himself was what he had been seeking.

☞ 30 ☜

After serving as the abbot of the Gyume Tantric College for six years and then as abbot of the Dalai Lama's Namgyal Dratsang monastery for fourteen, Rinpoche retired from monastic activity due to a heart condition. He lived quietly, devoting his time to meditation and to receiving private students. One day he announced to one of his students that as he had been promising him for several years, he would give him, and any friends he wanted to invite, a formal instruction.

On the day of the event, the hall was set up in a formal manner. Fifteen minutes into the lecture, the student noticed that Rinpoche looked quite himself while speaking, even laughing and telling jokes. But when he stopped to let the translator speak, his face changed color and he would contract slightly, close his eyes, and recite the mantra with more vigor than usual. After observing this for a few minutes, the student leaned over and asked him if anything was wrong. "Well," Rinpoche replied calmly, "I'm having a heart attack." He then resumed his instruction as though nothing had happened. When the translator spoke next, the student asked with some urgency, "Goodness, shouldn't we stop the teaching immediately?" With a deep and penetrating look, he replied, "As you wish. We can either go on now or else finish some other time." The student quickly called a halt to the event and moved Rinpoche to his bed. He sat in meditation while several of his monks surrounded him and chanted in low, deep tones.

That evening he continued to sit in meditation without moving. The next day, when the student visited Rinpoche's home, he was informed by his attendant that he was not well enough to receive visitors. That night as the lama sat in meditation, his breathing and his heart stopped, but he did not show the full signs of death. He was engaged in *tuk-dam* [the practice of retreating into the heart]. For three days he sat like this, without manifesting the signs of death. Then his head fell to one side and the death process was complete. Such is the death of an accomplished yogi.

ᑫ 31 ᑐ

Zen Master Shunryu Suzuki called his students together as he lay dying of cancer and said:

> If when I die, the moment I'm dying, if I suffer that is all right, you know; that is suffering Buddha. No confusion in it. Maybe everyone will struggle because of the physical agony or spiritual agony, too. But that is all right, that is not a problem. We should be grateful to have a limited body... like mine, like yours. If you had a limitless life it would be a real problem for you.

We die, and we do not die.
—Shunryu Suzuki

ᑫ 32 ᑐ

At age eighty-three, the first Dalai Lama called his disciples to him in an assembly hall of the monastery and informed them that the time of his passing had come. Some pleaded with him to use his powers to extend his life span, others asked if they could not call for a physician or do anything to prevent his passing. When he replied that there was nothing to be done, they asked if they should read any special prayers after his death. He answered:

> Always bear the teachings of Buddha in mind and for the sake of all living beings apply them to the cultivation of

Shunryu Suzuki

your own mindstream. Remember the doctrines of Tashi Lhunpo Monastery. Make every effort to live, meditate and teach in accordance with the true teachings of Buddha. This alone can fulfill my wishes.

He then entered into tantric meditation. His breath ceased and his heart stopped beating, but he remained in meditation for thirty days without showing any signs of death. His body transformed from that of an old man into that of a youth, and emanated lights so radiant that few could bear even to look upon him.

⌒ 33 ⌒

Toward the end of her life, Gauribai, poet-saint of Gujarat, made her home in Kashi. Once day, upon emerging from seven days in *samadhi*, she told her niece that her end was near. She made known her wish to die on the banks of the Jamuna River where, according to the Puranas [mythological texts of India], the boy Dhruva had performed his great penance. She prophesied that her death would take place on Ramanavami, Rama's birthday. Raj Sundeersimha arranged to send her to the place she desired. Gauribai remained there in *samadhi* for a few days and then went to eternal peace on Ramanavami at the age of fifty.

⌒ 34 ⌒

When Dokuon was very sick, Tekisui came to ask after him. Entering the sickroom, he announced himself, and then straddled Dokuon. With his face almost touching Dokuon's, he said, "Well, how are you?"

"Sick," answered Dokuon.

"Think you'll pull through?"

"No."

Without another word, Tekisui got up and left.

A few days before Tekisui's own death, Keichu came from afar to ask about him. "I hear," he said to the porter, "the master is very sick."

"Yes, sir," said the porter.

"Here's a box of cakes for him. When you hand it to him, give him this message: 'You're old enough to die without regret.'" With that Keichu left..

When the porter brought the cakes to Tekisui and gave him Keichu's message, the master smiled sweetly, as if he had forgotten all pain.

⌒ 35 ⌒

Shri Tapasviji Maharaj had two enlarged glands that refused to heal surgically removed from his thighs, but with time he became progressively weaker. On the morning of October 12, 1955, when asked how he felt, he replied, "I am in a happy state." Around noon of the same day, he asked one of his disciples to read the Bhagavad Gita aloud continuously, which he did. At 3:30 PM, he opened his eyes and raised two fingers. The eighteen devotees around his bed understood that he would enter *mahasamadhi* in two hours. An hour later he opened his eyes again and looked around at everyone; he lifted one finger and all present understood one hour remained. At 5:00 PM, Maharaj weakly uttered a

From the day of my coming hither
Full seventy years have passed.
Now, setting out on my final path
My two legs trample the sky.

—Tsugen Jakurei
fourteenth-century Zen monk

word no one understood. When asked to repeat it, he opened his eyes and said, "Below." He was gently placed on the floor. Upon recovering his breath, he called for a young disciple named Satcha and whispered something in his ear. It seemed he was transmitting his final blessings to this young *sadhu* who had served him so faithfully for years. When Maharaj heard the clock strike 5:30 he said loudly, "*Ram-Ram bolo*" ["Repeat the name of Ram"]. Then he blessed all present by saying, "Bhagawan will do good to you all."

Although he had no bodily strength left, Maharaj took a breath and held it for a long time. Suddenly, unassisted, he sat up and quite easily assumed the lotus posture. All the devotees in the room observed him for a few moments with deep love and reverence. His eyes were extremely serene and luminous. Then, motionless and with his gaze fixed between the eyebrows, he uttered slowly and loudly the sacred syllable "*Om*" with his last breath.

⇝ 36 ⇜

On the holy day of Shivaratri in February 1938, Gaurima, one of the disciples of Sri Ramakrishna, said that the play of her life was drawing to a close. Toward evening she asked for the emblem of the god Damodara to be brought to her. On seeing it she said: "Beautiful. I see Him vividly with my eyes open and with my eyes closed. I see Him all the time." She kept the emblem on her head and then on her bosom, before handing it over to the head of the ashram. The next day she uttered "Guru Ramakrishna" three times, repeated the Lord's name, and at 8:15 PM passed away peacefully.

Shri Bodhendra was one of a lineage of Siddhas, or perfected masters, who lived in the Cauvery Delta from the sixteenth to the nineteenth century. Bodhendra attained *samadhi* in quite a mysterious manner. Every morning, after finishing his bath in the river, he used to bury himself in the river bed and enter into a yogic state. In the evening he would ask the children playing nearby to help dig him up. One full moon day in the year 1692, Sri Bodhendra assumed the yogic state that he used to enter every day on the river bed, and attained *samadhi*. When his disciples arrived at the site, a divine voice informed them that Sri Bodhendra had attained *samadhi* and instructed them to raise a building around the site of his *samadhi* and perform worship there every year.

One day in March of 818, Master Ling Mo took a bath, burned incense, sat in a meditative pose, and said to his monks: "The Dharmakaya remains perfectly tranquil while manifesting going forth and coming in. Thousands of sages come from the same origin, and numerous spirits return to the same One. I have scattered myself by saturation—why should this give cause for grief? Don't be troubled in your spirits, but maintain right thought. If you follow this instruction of mine, you will really repay me for my favor; but if you act contrary to my advice, you are not my sons."

One monk asked, "To what place will you go, master?"

He answered, "I go to nowhere."

The monk asked, "Why can I not see you?"

The master said, "I am not that which can be seen by physical eyes."

These were his last words.

⁓ 39 ⁔

Sadasiva Brahmendra, an eighteenth-century Siddha who lived in the Cauvery Delta, became a *mouni* [one who takes a vow of silence] and an *avadhuta* [one who sheds all social convention, including the wearing of clothing]. By means of his occult powers, he informed his disciples of his desire to take *samadhi* along the banks of the Cauvery River. On the appointed day, he instructed them to build a cave, enclose him inside of it, and seal it. When one disciple voiced hesitation at this plan, Brahmendra assured him he would not go away but would continue to give his blessing from there. The disciples followed his command and his request that he be covered with *vilvam* leaves, sacred ash, camphor, and mud. Nine days after this event, a *vilvam* tree sprouted from his *samadhi*. On the same day, devotees at Varanasi and Manmadurai had visions of his entering *samadhi*. Some think this indicates that he shed his physical body at three different places at once.

⁓ 40 ⁔

Maharshi Brahmanda, after performing a particular *yajna* [ritual fire sacrifice], told his attendant the day of the month in February 1906 that he planned to leave the world. He was given *sannyas* [vows of renunciation] and then sat absorbed in a yogic posture for two days. He passed away in this way. His body was placed in a wooden box and, as planned, thrown into the sacred Narmada River while Vedic chants were being recited.

The next day a group of local tribesmen spotted him walking on the banks of the Narmada as they were approaching the town of Gangonath. Upon arriving in town, they were amazed to hear he had taken *samadhi* and been immersed in the mother Narmada the day before.

Awareness of death is the very bedrock of the path.
Until you have developed this awareness,
all other practices are obstructed.

—The Dalai Lama

⌒ 41 ⌒

When Zen Master Nan-ch'uan was about to die, a monk asked him, "Where will you go for the next hundred years?"

The master replied, "I will be reborn in the ox of a village farmer."

The monk asked, "May I follow you, Master?"

The master answered, "If you are coming with me, you had better bring some blades of grass in your mouth."

One morning in December of 834, Nan-ch'uan spoke the following words: "The star has been fading and the lamp growing dim for a long time. Do not say that I came or went." Just as he ceased speaking, he passed away.

⌐ 42 ⌐

When Zen Master Shen-t'san was preparing to depart this life, he shaved his head, bathed himself, and had the temple bell sounded to summon the congregation and announce his departure.

Then he asked, "Brothers, do you understand the voiceless *samadhi*?"

Those assembled answered, "No, we do not."

The master said, "Listen quietly, without cherishing any ideas."

With the congregation on the very tiptoe of expectation that they would hear about the voiceless *samadhi*, Master Shen-ts'an withdrew from the world.

⌐ 43 ⌐

Certain Tibetan yogins have mastered the winds, or inner air, that flows through the *chakras* or energy centers of the subtle body. One day one such accomplished being, a retreat master at a monastery in Kham, asked his attendant: "I am going to die now, so would you please look in the calendar for an auspicious date." The attendant was stunned, but did not dare contradict his master. He looked in the calendar and told him that the following Monday was a day when all the stars were auspicious. "Monday is three days away. Well, I think I can make it," the master replied. When his attendant came back into his room a few

moments later, he found the master sitting upright in yogic meditation posture, so still that it looked as though he had passed
away. There was no breathing, but a faint pulse was perceptible.
He decided not to do anything, but to wait. At noon he suddenly
heard a deep exhalation, and the master returned to his normal
condition, talked with his attendant in a joyful mood, and asked
for his lunch, which he ate with relish. He had been holding his
breath for the whole of the morning session of meditation. The
master knew that the human life span is counted as a finite number of breaths, and since he was near the end of these, he held his
breath so that the final number would not be reached until the
auspicious day. Just after lunch, the master took another deep
breath, and held it until the evening. He did the same the next
day, and the day after. When Monday came, he asked: "Is today
the auspicious day?" "Yes" replied the attendant. "Fine, I shall go
today," concluded the master. That day, without visible illness or
difficulty, the master passed away in his meditation.

☞ 44 ☜

Master Yin Feng addressed the assembly as follows: "Masters in
many places have died either sitting or lying down. These I have
witnessed myself. Did anyone ever pass away standing?"

A member of the assembly replied, "Yes, there was someone."

The master asked, "Was there anyone who was standing
upside-down when he took his last breath?"

The congregation answered, "If so, we have never heard of it."

The master then passed away standing upside-down, with his
robe still miraculously draping his body. When his followers

made their plans for carrying his body to be cremated, it was still immovable and people streamed in from far and near to see it.

The master had a sister who was a nun. Happening to be in the vicinity, she came right up to him and scolded, "Old brother, for ages you've been flouting the law, and you must even puzzle people after you are dead!" She gave him a shove with her hand, and he wobbled and fell flat on the ground.

At last he was cremated, and the ashes were collected and put into a pagoda.

⌒ 45 ⌒

When the tenth-century Chinese Zen Master named Dasui Fazhen was asked, "How are you at the time when life-death arrives?" he answered promptly, "When served tea, I take tea; when served a meal, I take a meal."

⌒ 46 ⌒

In the summer of 1983, Kyabje Ling Rinpoche, senior tutor to His Holiness the Dalai Lama, gave a week-long teaching to five of his closest Western disciples. One of them, Jhampa Shaneman, recalls the topic as being one most precious to Ling Rinpoche: *bodhicitta*, or the altruistic wish to gain enlightenment for the benefit of all sentient beings. Shortly afterward, he suffered the first in a series of small stokes. On Christmas Day of that year, four of the disciples spontaneously gathered together at Ling Rinpoche's house in the foothills of the Himalayas. While sitting in his downstairs room rejoicing over their chance meeting, they were

Kyabje Ling Rinpoche

informed that he had just passed away. That he should pass away on this date bore special significance for them: Ling Rinpoche had always been fond of honoring—and taking rest on—Christian holidays. He was eighty-one years old.

In death, Ling Rinpoche's exceptional spiritual attainment was made quite evident. He died lying on his right side in a special meditation posture modeled on the posture the Buddha assumed at *parinirvana* [his passage from this world]. In the Tibetan tradition the body of a dead person is left on the deathbed for at least three days in order to allow the stream of consciousness to leave the body peacefully. Several techniques can be utilized during the death experience if one is an accomplished meditator. With these techniques, the body does not show any signs of deterioration as long as the consciousness remains in it. If the person has the requisite skill, such a meditation can continue for many days. Ling Rinpoche maintained a technique called the Meditation on the Clear Light of Death for a total of thirteen days. The Swiss disciple who cared for him during the last weeks of his life visited his room daily to make sure everything was satisfactory. She confirmed that during this entire time Ling Rinpoche's face remained beautiful and flesh-toned, and his body showed none of the normal signs of death. Only a small number of great masters from Tibet have been able to achieve this extraordinary state.

His Holiness the Dalai Lama was so moved by the spirituality of his personal teacher that he decided to have Ling Rinpoche's body embalmed instead of cremated. Today the statue holding the remains of Kyabje Ling Rinpoche may be viewed at the palace of the Dalai Lama in Dharamsala.

❧ 47 ❧

Tao-ch'o had a grave illness at age sixty-five. Feeling himself to be dying, he suddenly had a vision of his master, T'an-luan, who commanded him to continue teaching. It is recorded that T'an-luan's voice was heard and heavenly flowers were seen by all present. From that moment on, Tao ch'o quickly recovered, gained a new set of teeth, and was revered like a god by his disciples. He continued to preach for eighteen more years before his death.

❧ 48 ❧

Seng-chi had a dream while he was very ill that the Buddha of light took him through the void of the whole universe. He awoke free from all signs of disease and suffering. The next night he searched for his sandals, said that he must leave, and then lay down and died, staring into the void with joyful anticipation on his face.

❧ 49 ❧

According to his biography, Ikkyu did not distinguish between the high and low in society, and he enjoyed mingling with artisans, merchants, and children. Youngsters followed him about, and birds came to eat out of his hands. Whatever possessions he received, he passed on to others. He was strict and demanding but treated all without favoritism.

Near the end of his life, Ikkyu told his disciples, "After my death some of you will seclude yourselves in the forests and

Seventy-six years,
Unborn, undying:
Clouds break up,
Moon sails on

—Tokken (1244–1319)
Japanese Zen master

mountains to meditate, while others may drink *sake* and enjoy the company of women. Both kinds of Zen are fine, but if some become professional clerics, babbling about 'Zen as the Way,' they are my enemies."

✿ 50 ✽

Swami Vivekananda, one of Sri Ramakrishna's greatest disciples, approaching the end said: "A great *tapasya* and meditation has come upon me, and I am making ready for death."

His disciples couldn't help but remember the words delivered by Sri Ramakrishna many years earlier, following Vivekananda's *nirvikalpa samadhi*: "Now the Mother has shown you everything. But this realization, like the jewel locked in a box, will be hidden away from you and kept in my custody. I will keep the key with me. Only after you have fulfilled your mission on this earth will the box be unlocked, and you will know everything as you have known now."

As Vivekenanda approached death, his disciples remembered his experience in the cave at Amarnath in 1898; at that time he received the grace of Shiva not to die until he himself willed it. As his guru had done before him, Vivekenanda consulted the Bengali almanac before his death to help determine the day he should discard his mortal shell.

Three days before he left, Vivekananda pointed out the site on the monastery grounds where he wanted to be cremated. On the July 4, 1902, he awoke early and meditated for three hours. Later the same morning he asked a disciple to read a passage from the Yajurveda. Although he normally ate alone because of his illness, that day he partook in the community meal with great relish. He then gave Sanskrit grammar lessons for three hours and took a long walk with another swami. At seven in the evening he retired to his room to meditate alone. Following his meditation, he called a disciple and asked him to open all the windows and fan his head. As he lay quietly on his bed, his attendant thought he was sleeping or meditating. At the end of an hour he breathed once, very deeply. After a few minutes, he did so again; his eyes became fixed between his eyebrows and his face assumed a divine expression. A brother disciple noted that a little blood was visible in his nostrils, around his mouth, and in his eyes. According to Yogic scriptures, the life breath of an illumined yogi passes out through the opening at the top of the head. As it does so, it causes the blood to flow into the nostrils and the mouth.

The "great ecstasy" of Swami Vivekenanda occurred at the age of thirty-nine, fulfilling his own prophecy that he would not live to be forty years old.

~ 51 ~

After having spent twenty-nine fruitful years in a cave in strict retreat, the Tibetan nun Jetsunla was known to some as the wish-fulfilling gem. In 1959 she had to break her retreat and leave Tibet. Her cousin built her a small mud and grass hut, large enough to hold Jetsunla and two visitors. Revered as the highest lama of the area, she would receive devotees the first nine days of each month and meditate the rest of the time. A few months before she passed away she said: "Now I have accomplished what I had to do and achieved everything that I need to. Now I don't have to live any longer. I am very happy if I can go soon, but before I go I must see His Holiness the Dalai Lama, because I have a few words to say to him." About a month later His Holiness visited Orissa and conferred privately with her for over an hour. She came out from this meeting very happy and said: "Now my last wish is fulfilled, now I am free to go." Soon after, Jetsunla became slightly ill and, while remaining in meditation posture, she passed away.

Another Tibetan nun related that when Jetsunla died, the air was filled with a sweet scent, and the sounds of cymbals could be heard. And at the time of her cremation, the sky was filled with rainbows.

~ 52 ~

One spring day in 1995, after spending a month instructing Soto Zen teachers near San Francisco, Maezumi Roshi returned to Japan to visit family and friends, as had been his custom for twenty-five years. During his visit, in the presence of an old friend and abbot, he completed and dated—"in the month of the Azaleas"—the *inka* [final statement of empowerment from master to successor] for his disciple, Sensei Tetsugen Glassman. This document, which turned out to be his "last Dharma words," concludes as follows:

> *Life after life, birth after birth, please practice diligently.*
> *Never falter.*
> *Do not let die the Wisdom seed of the Buddhas and Ancestors.*
> *Truly! I implore you!*

Hakuyu Taizan Maezumi

❧ 53 ❧

Hui-yung, in the throes of a grave illness in 414, suddenly asked for his clothes and sandals, folded his hands, and tried to stand, as if he were seeing something. When the attendant monks asked him what he saw, he replied, "The Buddha is coming." Just as he finished speaking, he died.

❧ 54 ❧

By 1693, Bankei's health had so deteriorated that his disciples began building him a burial pagoda. On the tenth of August Bankei was carried there on a litter. The next day he told an attendant in secret that he would be dead within three months. For the time left to him, Bankei continued seeing students from his bed. Immediately before he died in November, as he'd predicted, he stopped taking food and medicine. Giving instructions to his most intimate students, he admonished them for their tears, saying, "How do you expect to see me, if you look at me in terms of birth and death?" When one disciple asked him to compose a traditional Zen death poem, he said:

> I've lived for seventy-two years. I've been teaching people for forty-five. What I've been telling you and others every day during that time is all my death verse. I'm not going to make another one now, before I die, just because everyone else does it.

Having said this, the great Zen master passed away, sitting perfectly straight. Over five thousand people were in attendance at his funeral.

ᕾ 55 ᕦ

After two years in the rock cave near his hometown of Hsiang-yang, P'ang Yun—also known as Layman P'ang—decided it was time to die. Sitting for meditation, he instructed his daughter Ling-chao to go outside and come back to inform him when the sun had reached its zenith. At twelve, he would die. Ling-chao went out and came back almost immediately, saying, "It's already noon, and there's an eclipse of the sun. Come and look."

"Is that so?" said P'ang.

"Oh, yes."

P'ang Yun rose from his seat and went to the window. At that moment Ling-chao jumped into his vacant place, crossed her legs, and, instantly, died. When P'ang returned and saw what had happened, he said, "My daughter's way was always quick. Now she's gone ahead of me." He went out, gathered firewood, performed a cremation ceremony, and observed the traditional mourning period of seven days before dying himself in the company of Governor Yu Ti. Yu had come to ask how he was. P'ang put his head on his friend's knee, saying, "I beg you to just see all existent phenomena as empty and to beware of taking as real all that is nonexistent. Take care of yourself in this world of shadows and echoes." Then he peacefully passed away.

ᕾ 56 ᕦ

Six months before Lahiri Mahasaya left his physical body he told his wife, "The body will go soon. Do not cry at that time." During the summer of 1895, the master developed a small boil on his

Four and fifty years
I've hung the sky with stars
Now I leap through—
What shattering!

—Dogen (1200–1253)
Japanese Zen master

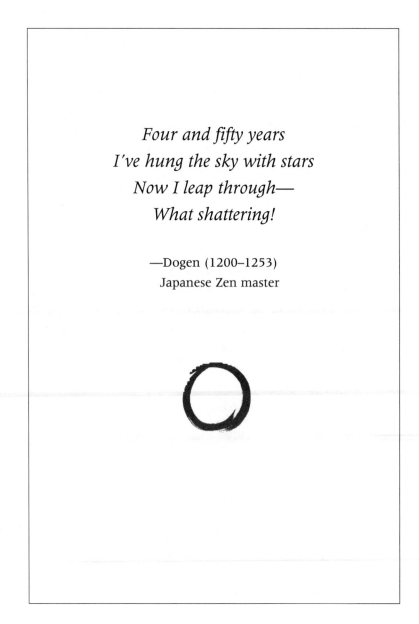

back, which he did not want lanced. Some of those near him thought perhaps he was working out in his own body the negative karma of some of his disciples. When a few disciples became insistent, he replied cryptically: "The body has to find a cause to go. I will be agreeable to whatever you want to do."

A few days before his final departure, disciples of Lahiri Mahasaya gathered around him. Some, having been called internally, arrived from long distances. For hours the master expounded on the Bhagavad Gita, then he simply said: "I am going home." This remark provoked an outpouring of anguish among his devotees. He responded with: "Be comforted. I shall rise again." Following this statement, Lahiri Mahasaya rose from his seat and walked in a circle three times. He then assumed the lotus posture, facing north, and gloriously entered the final *mahasamadhi*.

Death arises from life itself.

—Lao Tzu

☞ *57* ☜

Just before Chih-hsien of Huanch'i passed away in 905 AD he asked his attendants, "Who dies sitting?" They answered, "A monk." He said, "Who dies standing?" They replied, "Enlightened monks." He then walked around seven steps with his hands hanging down, and died.

⪻ 58 ⪼

When Zen Master Ryoen Genseki was told he had cancer and was given a life expectancy of several months, he set off alone on a long pilgrimage. Ryoen lived for two more years. For nearly two weeks before his death, in critical condition, every morning he crawled from his room to the main hall of the temple to invoke the names of the masters of his lineage. He needed to rest frequently throughout both his crawling and invocation. When he died, he was found sitting in the *zazen* position.

⪻ 59 ⪼

Once when his village was beset by wolves, Dokyo sat for seven nights in different graveyards to test his *samadhi* while wolves sniffed at his throat. At the age of eighty, Dokyo wrote these last words while seated in the upright Zen position.

> *In the frantic hurry of dying*
> *It's difficult to utter the last words.*
> *If I were to speak a wordless word,*
> *I wouldn't speak, I wouldn't speak.*

Then he put down his brush, hummed "an ancient song" to himself, suddenly laughed heartily, and died.

⪻ 60 ⪼

For many years Daito Kokushi had been unable to meditate in the full lotus position because of a crippled leg. When he felt death approaching, he broke his leg with his own hands and took the full lotus. Then, despite agonizing pain, he wrote his final words and died with the last stroke of the brush.

> *Buddhas and patriarchs cut to pieces;*
> *The sword is ever kept sharpened.*
> *Where the wheel turns*
> *The void gnashes its teeth.*

⌐ 61 ⌐

In the year 1582, the abbot of Yerin-ji, Kwaisen, refused to hand over soldiers who were seeking refuge at his temple. He and his monks were locked in a tower that was then set ablaze. In their usual manner, they sat in *zazen*, and the abbot gave his last sermon: "We are surrounded by flames. How would you revolve your Wheel of Dharma at this critical moment?" Each then expressed his understanding. When all were finished, the abbot gave his view: "For peaceful meditation, we need not go to the mountains and streams. When thoughts are quiet, fire itself is cool and refreshing." They perished without a sound.

⌐ 62 ⌐

When Eshun, a Zen nun, was past sixty and about to leave this world, she had some monks pile up some wood in the monastery courtyard. Seating herself firmly in the middle of the pile of wood, she had it set on fire around the edges. "O nun!" shouted a monk, "Is it hot in there?"

"Such a matter would concern only a stupid person like your-self," answered Eshun. The flames arose, and she died.

⤙ 63 ⤚

When Master Fugai sensed that death was near, he had one of the monks dig a deep pit. The master then climbed into it and, standing there with immense dignity, directed the monk to cover him with earth.

⤙ 64 ⤚

As Swami Brahmananda was in the process of dying, he placed his hand on one of his disciples and said: "Do not grieve. You have served me well. You shall be merged in God and reach knowledge of Brahman. I give you my blessing that you may attain this."

Then he called all the disciples and devotees who were present to his side. For each he had a blessing and an affectionate word. He then became absorbed in his transcendental vision and, after some time, continued in a sweet, tender voice: "I am floating. I am floating on the leaf of faith and knowledge on the ocean of Brahman." Then suddenly he exclaimed that he saw others who had passed away before him: Sri Ramakrishna, Vivekananda, Premananda, Yogananda. He was still for a while, absorbed in meditation with an expression of great sweetness on his face. Out of the silence, he suddenly exclaimed: "Ah, that inexpressible light! Ramakrishna, the Krishna of my Ramakrishna... I am the shepherd boy. Put anklets on my feet; I want to dance with my

Brahmananda

Krishna. I want to hold his hand—the little boy Krishna... Ah, Krishna, my Krishna, you have come! Krishna... Krishna... Can't you see him? Haven't you eyes to see? Oh, how beautiful! My Krishna... on the lotus... eternal... the Sweet One!

"My play is over now. Look! The child Krishna is caressing me. He is calling me to come away with him! I am coming..." A deep stillness and holiness seemed to vibrate in the large hall where Brahmananda was lying and uttering these words.

His physical condition worsened and on the evening of the third day, his chest suddenly heaved. It was as if a great wave of breath passed up the body to the throat. His half-closed eyes opened, and he gazed into the distance, his eyes shining with magnificent brilliance. Thus it was that, on April 10, 1922, the life left his body.

~ 65 ~

On March 6, 1952, Paramahansa Yogananda told his disciples laughingly, "I have a big day tomorrow. Wish me luck." The next day he attended a banquet at Los Angeles' Biltmore Hotel for the new Indian ambassador. He did not gaze about with his usual heart-warming smile. After eating modestly, the guru rose to make a speech about "spiritual India." He spoke more slowly and in a more measured cadence than usual. Yogananda ended his talk with a quotation from one of his own poems:

> *Where Ganges, woods, Himalayan caves,*
> *and men dream God—*
> *I am hallowed; my body touched that sod.*

Paramahansa Yogananda

As he finished, Paramahansa lifted his eyes, turned slightly to the right and slid to the floor. The great guru's outward mission was finished.

Officials who conducted the embalming of the body reported an unusual phenomenon: No physical disintegration was visible, even twenty days after death. Yogananda's body was apparently devoid of impurities. They reported this case as being unique in their experience.

Death is only an experience through which you are
meant to learn a great lesson: you cannot die.
—Paramahansa Yogananda

⌒ 66 ⌒

Nampo Shomyo, also known as Daio Kokushi, studied in China and brought the Yogi line of Rinzai Zen to Japan. Upon his installation as head abbot of an important temple at the age of seventy-two, he said to his disciples, "Today I'm here, coming from nowhere. Exactly one year from today I'll go, without having anywhere to go." Exactly a year later, he wrote this poem, and died.

I tongue-lashed wind and rain,
Above Buddhas, Patriarchs.
Lightning's no match for mind.

☞ 67 ☜

Master Kanzan Egen started teaching at sixty, never lectured, and accepted only a few students, whom he trained with extreme severity. Among the few koans he used, his favorite was "For Egen, here there is no birth-and-death." On the day of his death, he entrusted his affairs to his sole heir and dressed himself in his traveling clothes. He then went out from the abbot's quarters and, standing quietly and alone beside the "wind and water pond" at the front gate of the temple, he passed away.

☞ 68 ☜

While sitting in meditation, and just after having said aloud for the benefit of his disciples, "No suppressing arrival, no following departure," Daibai heard a weasel shriek, the "this" of the following poem. It is said that on reciting it he indeed breathed his last.

> *I'm at one with this, this only.*
> *You, my disciples,*
> *Uphold it firmly.*
> *Now I can breathe my last.*

☞ 69 ☜

On the first of December of his sixty-sixth year, Etsugan announced to his disciples, "Well, I've made up my mind to die on the eighth, the day of Buddha's awakening. If you've any questions, better ask them before then."

As the master continued to carry out all his religious duties, however, some of the monks suspected that he was having a bit of fun with them, while others were struck with grief.

On the evening of the seventh there was nothing out of the ordinary, but that night Etsugan called them all together and taught them about Shakyamuni's enlightenment. He also entrusted his affairs to them.

At daybreak he took a bath and then, while sitting dignified in Zen meditation, recited his last poem:

> *Buddha came down from the mountain,*
> *I ascended it. Always I've*
> *Run counter to his teaching,*
> *And now I'm bound for hell—ha-ha!*
> *Man's inquisitiveness is sheer nonsense.*

He then closed his eyes and, still sitting, died.

⌐ 70 ⌐

When Master P'u-hua sensed that his end was near, he announced to the people of the nearby town that he would go the next day to the Eastern Gate and die there. The whole community went in a procession behind him and assembled outside the city wall to pay their respects. P'u-hua then announced: "A funeral today would not be in accord with the Blue Crow [a mythological bird]. I will pass away tomorrow at the Southern Gate." The next day the people followed him again, but he announced, "It would be more auspicious to leave by the Western Gate tomorrow." On the third day fewer people came, and he decided on the North Gate instead. On the fourth day he picked up his own coffin and carried it out of the Northern Gate. Shaking his bell, he entered the coffin and passed away

～ 71 ～

When the great Tibetan master Jamyang Khyentse Rinpoche, sometimes called the "master of masters," fell ill he was on pilgrimage in Sikkim. All the senior lamas, the heads of the lineages, arrived one after another to visit him, and prayers and rituals for his long life went on day and night. His disciples pleaded with him to continue living, for it is said a master of his greatness has the power to decide when it is time to leave his body. As he lay in bed, accepting all the offerings, he laughed and replied: "All right, just to be auspicious, I'll say I will live." But the first indication he was going to die came through the Gyalwang Karmapa, whom he had told he had completed the work he had come to do in this life, and he had decided to leave this world. His death was to occur just after news came that the three great monasteries of Tibet—Sera, Drepung, and Ganden—had been occupied by the Chinese.

Ten days before he passed away, the ground was shaken by an enormous earthquake. According the Buddhist sutras, this is a sign that marks the imminent passing of an enlightened being. Jamyang Khyentse died at three o'clock in the morning on the sixth day of the fifth Tibetan month in 1959.

In certain traditions, during the time a master remains in meditation after death it is important to maintain secrecy. For three days after he passed, complete secrecy was kept; no one was allowed to know that Khyentse had died, simply that his health

Jamyang Khyentse Rinpoche

had taken a turn for the worse. On the third day after he had medically died, he came out of meditation: his nose suddenly deflated, the color in his face drained away, and his head fell slightly to one side. Until that moment there had been a certain poise and strength to his body. After the body was washed and dressed and taken to the main temple of the palace, crowds filed in to show their respect. Then hundreds of people in amazement reported seeing an incandescent, milky light that gradually spread everywhere. Even the four electric lamps outside were dimmed by this mysterious light. One of the other masters explained that such manifestations of light are said to be a sign of someone attaining Buddhahood.

⟜ 72 ⟝

Hyma, together with her mother, a realized yogini named Anasuya, lived in Jillellamudi in the mid-twentieth century. At the age of twenty-five, Hyma became critically ill with smallpox. At the last moment of her life she called out loudly, "Amma [Mother], I am coming!" A *samadhi* shrine was prepared for Hyma. Anasuya cleaned the body and placed it in the *samadhi* pit in *siddhasana* [a yoga posture]. While the entire community stood by weeping, Anasuya seemed strangely cheerful. She sat beside the grave and smiled at the onlookers. Then she signaled to a doctor standing nearby. He examined Hyma's body and was shocked to find it quite hot, with a faint trace of respiration. He had just climbed out of the pit when the group standing nearby felt an electric jolt. The doctor reentered the grave and discovered blood oozing from Hyma's fontanel. In the yogic scriptures, it is written that at death an open fontanel is a sign that the soul has left the body through the *sahasrara chakra*, the "divine exit" at the top of the head, and become liberated.

Death is nothing but a gateway to birth.
Nothing that lives ever dies, it only changes form.
When a man's body is weary the soul leaves
the body to receive newer and fresher garments.
And so on goes this great play of God—
from eternity to eternity.
—Guru Nanak

⌐ 73 ⌐

When news spread that Guru Nanak was ready to embark on his last journey, the disciples began to descend upon Kartarpur, on the banks of the Ravi River, to see him. While seated under an acacia tree, his wife, disciples, and successor—Guru Angad—all began to cry; He pacified them, saying they shouldn't weep. He then uttered a long hymn and the assembly began to chant. Then Guru Nanak went into a trance and recited a poem that describes the intense longing of the soul for union with the Lord.

During the last moments of his life, the Muslims were saying, "We shall bury him" while the Hindus said, "We shall cremate him." The guru responded to this saying: "Put ye flowers on both sides—those of the Hindus on the right and of the Muslims on the left. They whose flowers remain fresh will have the choice."

He then asked the congregation to recite God's praises. As the epilogue to the hymn was being read, the Guru Nanak pulled the sheet over himself and lay down. The assembly paid obeisance. When the sheet was lifted, there was nothing but flowers. The Hindus and Muslims, equally astonished, took their respective flower offerings and the entire assembly fell to their knees. The date was September 7, 1539.

⌒ 74 ⌒

As Master Xu Yun grew weaker during the course of a grave illness, he was urged to seek a doctor's care but he declined, saying, "My causal link with this world is coming to an end." Upon thanking his disciples for helping to rebuild a monastery with him, the master gave them the following instruction: "After my death, please have my body dressed in my yellow robe and garments, placed in a coffin a day later, and cremated at the foot of the hill to the west of the cowshed. Please then mix my ashes with sugar, flour, and oil, knead all this into nine balls and throw them into the river as an offering to living beings in the water. If you help me to fulfill my vow, I shall be eternally grateful." When asked for his last words, the master replied: "Practice *sila*, *dhyana*, and *prajna* [discipline, meditation, and wisdom] to wipe out desire, anger, and stupidity." After a pause, he continued, "Develop the right thought and right mind to create the great spirit of fearlessness for the deliverance of men and the whole world. You are tired, please retire to rest."

A few moments before the master departed this world he implored them to preserve the faith. "How to preserve it? The

Xu Yun

answer is in the word *sila*." After saying this he brought his palms together and enjoined upon his assistants to take good care of themselves. They left the room and returned an hour later to find that Xu Yun had quietly passed away. He was 120 years of age. When his body was cremated, the air was filled with a rare fragrance and a white smoke went up into the sky. In the ashes were found over a hundred relics of five different colors and countless small ones, which were mostly white.

⌒ 75 ⌒

When it came time to die on July 19, 1888, Yamaoka Tesshu bathed and put on a spotless white kimono. Following convention, his disciples requested a death verse. Tesshu immediately chanted this haiku:

> *Tightening my abdomen*
> *against the pain—*
> *The caw of a morning crow*

Since his disciples had never heard of a death verse with the word "pain" in it—they thought "peace," "light," or a similar sentiment would be more appropriate for a Zen master—they were hesitant to make it public. With trepidation, they gave the verse to the Abbot Gasan when he asked for it. "What a magnificent death verse," he exclaimed. When the crow flew past and cried out, Tesshu was hemorrhaging, his stomach eaten away by his cancer—those two events filled the cosmos.

Tesshu placed himself in formal *zazen* posture, bid his family and friends goodbye ("Don't worry about food or clothing," he cautioned his eldest son), closed his eyes, took a deep breath, and entered eternal meditation. He was fifty-three years old. Tekisui, abbot of Tenryuji, composed this verse for Tesshu's funeral:

> *Sword and brush poised between the Absolute*
> *and the Relative,*
> *His loyal courage and noble strength pierced the Heavens.*
> *A dream of fifty-three years,*
> *Enveloped by the pure fragrance of a lotus*
> *blooming in the midst of a roaring fire.*

⤙ 76 ⤚

Over the years, Sri Aurobindo had developed an enlarged prostate. Late in 1950, he entered into a deep coma, due to an extreme uremic condition. Before entering the coma, he refused any major treatment and declined to use his therapeutic power on himself. Asked why, he said simply, "Can't explain, you won't understand."

Medically this condition normally does not permit voluntary return to consciousness. To the surprise of his attending doctors, Sri Aurobindo opened his eyes at frequent intervals and asked for a drink of water or inquired as to the time. This led many to believe that the coma was coexisting with a conscious yogic withdrawal from the body. He spoke to his attendant, and even kissed those faithful companions of his last years. A half an hour before his heart stopped, Sri Aurobindo looked out from his calm compassionate eyes, and spoke the name of the doctor by his side, and drank some water.

Yamaoka Tesshu

Shivapuri Baba

He passed away in the early hours of December 5, 1950. A few days later the Mother [Sri Aurobindo's wife] announced: "The funeral of Sri Aurobindo has not taken place today. His body is charged with such a concentration of supramental light that there is no sign of decomposition, and the body will be kept lying on his bed so long as it remains intact." In the late afternoon of December 9, he was buried simply in a vault specially prepared in the center of the ashram courtyard.

⌒ 77 ⌒

As his last days approached, Kukai, also known as Kobo Daishi, sat absorbed in meditation and refused food. This great founder of the Shingon sect of esoteric Buddhism had prophesied that his death would come on the twenty-first day of the third month. Not long before he died, he told his disciples: "My life will not last much longer. Live harmoniously and preserve with care the teachings of the Buddha. I am returning to the mountain to remain there forever." The great transformation—ordinarily called death—took place within Kobo Daishi as he was lying on his right side. He breathed his last on the twenty-first day of the third month of 835.

⌒ 78 ⌒

A most remarkable Indian Master from the state of Kerala, Shivapuri Baba, is said to have been born with a smile on his lips. He graced this earth for 137 years, living 23 years in solitude, and spending nearly another half century traversing the globe on foot. His last words, which were given in a total conscious and lucid state, were: "Live right life, worship God. That is all. Nothing more." At 6:15 AM he got up, sat on his bed, asked for a drink, and said "I'm gone." He then laid himself down on his right side, resting his head on the palm of his right hand, and left his body.

If one wants to die peacefully,
one must begin helping oneself
long before one's time to die has come.
—Swami Muktananda

❧ 79 ❧

When the sixty-two-year-old Tsong Khapa was giving discourses at Drepung in the year 1419, those present saw rainbows appear in a clear sky, which they took as an indication of his impending death. During his teaching, Tsong Khapa unexpectedly halted halfway through, saying he would break there. This was a most unusual occurrence, and again people felt it to be an indication that he was preparing for his passing away. It is considered auspicious to leave a teaching unfinished if departing somewhere, to ensure that master and disciples will meet again and continue the teaching in this and future lives. From there he went to the great temple at Lhasa to make prayers and offerings. Before leaving the temple he prostrated, which normally is only done when return to a place will be impossible.

The next day he admitted he was in pain though it was not immediately obvious. He gave his hat and robe to one of his disciples and offered advice to those present about the importance of not drifting away from an altruistic state of mind.

On the twentieth of the tenth month, Tsong Khapa made an extensive offering to the deity Heruka and that night meditated on the Adamantine Recitation, a special tantric breathing exercise. Very early the morning of the twenty-fifth, sitting in full lotus, he meditated on emptiness. At dawn he made a series of inner offerings, although no one present could understand why. Then his breathing ceased and his body regained the vibrancy of a sixteen-year-old. Many disciples present witnessed the emission of variegated light rays from his body, which substantiated the belief that Tsong Khapa entered the realm of enlightened beings.

Oracles were consulted to find the most appropriate treatment for the body. When they prophesied that it should be enshrined in a stupa, a special hall was built to hold a silver platform topped with a sold gold stupa. His mummified body was amazingly still intact in the middle of this century. Tsong Khapa was praised by the ninth Karmapa as one "who swept away wrong views with the correct and perfect ones."

◠ 80 ◠

In 1215, Eisai, one of the founders of Japanese Zen, knew just when his death was approaching. He journeyed to Kyoto to "show people how to die." Upon his arrival, he first preached to the crowd, then sat completely still in the upright Zen position,

Leaving, where to go?
Staying, where?
Which to choose? I stand aloof.
To whom to speak my parting words?
The galaxy, white, immense.
A crescent moon.

—Shoten
eleventh-century Chinese Zen master

and died. However, when his followers complained that his death had been too sudden, he revived. He died for good in the same manner five days later.

⌒ 81 ⌒

As Ninakawa lay dying Zen Master Ikkyu visited him,

"Shall I lead you on?" Ikkyu asked.

Ninakawa replied: "I came here alone and I go alone. What help could you be to me?"

Ikkyu answered: "If you think you really come and go, that is your delusion. Let me show you the path on which there is no coming and going."

With his words, Ikkyu had revealed the path so clearly that Ninakawa smiled and passed away.

⌒ 82 ⌒

When Rumi's time of death drew near, he cautioned his disciples to have no fear or anxiety on his account. He told them to remember him "so that I may show myself to you, in whatever form that may be, and... ever be shedding in your breasts the light of heavenly inspiration."

As he lay in extreme sickness, severe earthquakes took place for seven days and nights. On the seventh day, in response to the alarm of his disciples, he calmly remarked: "Poor earth! It is eager for a fat morsel! It shall have one!"

After his death, Rumi's body was laid on his bier and washed by a loving disciple. Every drop of this ablution water was caught and drunk with reverence by his disciples as the holiest of waters. As the washer folded Rumi's arms over his breast, a tremor appeared to pass over the inert body and the washer fell with his face on the lifeless breast, weeping. Upon feeling his ear pulled by the dead saint's hand, as an admonition, he passed into a swoon. In this state he heard a cry from heaven, which said to him: "The saints of the Lord have nothing to fear, neither shall they sorrow. Believers die not; they merely depart from one habitation to another abode."

The funeral procession was attended by mourners of all creeds—Turks, Christians, Jews, Romans, and Arabs. Each group recited sacred scriptures according to their own traditions. Rumi belonged to everyone.

ᴄ 83 ᴐ

Early in May of 1963 Sivananda began a rigorous tape recording session that lasted for days. He did this for hours, unmindful of the strain. During one of these sessions he said aloud, "The sight is getting dim; take whatever you want now. The hearing is getting dull; tell whatever you want to tell, now itself. The tongue is getting inarticulate; ask whatever you want to ask."

On June 21, he develop a pain in his hip, and on this rare occasion did not attend the *satsang*. At night the pain grew more intense. On a subsequent day, despite illness, Sivananda began dictating as usual. After a few sentences he paused and said quietly, "Happiness comes when the individual merges in God." Then there was a long pause. This was the last recorded message of Swami Sivananda.

Sivananda

Despite the suffering of his physical body over the next few weeks, Sivananda was never dejected; his spirit was joyful and all who went near him during his last illness felt his irresistible love flowing out and encompassing them. On the evening of July 14 he developed a fever. For some time he had difficulty swallowing. His disciples wanted to give him barley water, as was the usual practice, but he insisted on Ganges water. It was brought to him and he had no difficulty in swallowing half a glassful. And with that he departed from the body at 11:15 PM.

Sivananda's body was placed in the lotus posture as dazed and tearful disciples and devotees softly chanted on the verandah of his residence; members of the ashram went in to bow before the beloved form in silence. The next day messages of sympathy and condolence arrived at the Rishikesh post office from all over the world. On July 16, to the sound of conches and bells and Vedic mantras, the holy form of Sivananda was taken to the Ganges where it was ceremoniously bathed. It was then placed on a palanquin filled with flowers and borne in procession to the ashram area, where the ceremony of Arati was performed. To the recitation of holy mantras, Sivananda's body was taken in and tenderly placed in the *samadhi* shrine—its final resting place.

In his loving tribute, Venkatesananda wrote: "…He created an inside, and has entered it. Now he works inside, out of view, but more truly and purposefully active, therefore."

⌒ 84 ⁓

When Goei was on the verge of death, he made his ablutions and burned incense, then sat in the proper way and said to the monks, "The Body of the Law in Nirvana shows birth and death; the thousand Holy Ones are all the same basically; the ten thousand spirits all return to one. I am now disintegrating; why should I be foolish enough to grieve at that? Do not trouble your souls. Keep a true mind! If you obey these demands you are truly showing your gratitude to me. If you do not, you are not my children." At this moment a monk asked, "Where is our teacher going?" Goei answered, "I am going to No-place." The monk said, "Why shan't I be able to see you any more? Goei said, "That place is not one to be seen with human eyes," and passed away.

⌒ 85 ⌒

On the fifteenth day of the tenth month, Enni announced to his followers that he was about to die. They did not believe him. On the day of his death he ordered that the drum be beaten and his imminent death proclaimed. He sat down in his chair and wrote his last words. After adding the date and his signature, he wrote "Farewell" and died.

⌒ 86 ⌒

The Taoist master Chuang-tzu describes the death of Yu, a Taoist who went before him. When Yu fell ill, another sage named Szu went to visit him and asked how he fared. Yu said, "Wonderful. The way of the master is deforming me! My back is as crooked as a hunchback's and my organs are all topsy-turvy. My chin sticks in my navel, my shoulders rise up above my head and my pigtail points to the sky. The elements of nature must be all confused."

His heart was calm and his manner carefree. He limped to the well, looked at his reflection in the water and said, "My, my! How the Maker of Things is deforming me!" Szu asked, "Does this upset you?" "Why would it?" said Yu. "...I was born when it was time to be born, and I shall die when it is time to die. If we are in peace with time and follow the order of things, neither sorrow nor joy will move us. The ancients called this 'freedom from bondage.' Those who are entangled with the appearance of things cannot free themselves. But nothing can overcome the order of nature. Why should I be upset?"

⇢ 87 ⇣

Nogami Senryo lived the teachings of her master, Dogen, with her entire being. She went about life carefully and lovingly caring for the Seikanji nun's temple in Japan and training her one apprentice, Kuriki Kakujo. Nogami took care to steep Kuriki and those around her, but mostly herself, to approach everything in the spirit of the classical Zen dictum: "*Zadatsu Ryubo*. Die sitting. Die standing. This is the way of the monastic." In Zen these postures are considered absolute proof of enlightenment. Dogen used this dictum to stress that practice means to do all activities with steady attention to the reality of the present moment.

Nogami practiced this awareness each morning as she sped—with fingers extended on the damp, neatly folded rag—down the wooden floor in the hallway collecting each particle of dust, after each meal as she wiped her bowl clean with a piece of pickled radish, and every afternoon as she pulled tiny weeds from the white stone garden. Her body understood that enlightenment

Nogami Senryo

meant tolerating nothing less than the perfect completion of each activity. *"Zadatsu Ryubo*. Die Sitting. Die standing."* She repeated this like a mantra as she strove to live each moment with pure and relentless concentration.

On a crisp November afternoon in 1980, Nogami's adamantine voice pierced the silence: "It's time for *Zadatsu Ryubo!*" Her apprentice, Kuriki, not knowing what to expect, rushed to the dim hallway. There she saw Nogami slowly walking toward the bronze statue of Shakyamuni Buddha, sitting in full lotus on the altar in the Worship Hall. Arriving just in time to witness the stout, 97-year-old nun in simple black robes take a final step to perfect her stance, Kuriki pealed, "Congratulations!" as Nogami died standing.

✿ 88 ✽

Toward the end of her life, Gyanamata's physical condition had deteriorated to the point that she had to stay in bed most of the time. Another nun in the Ramakrishna order said of the twenty-two months she spent with her, "Sri Gyanamata was unable to even draw a breath without pain, yet she never complained about anything." It was reported that on Gyanamata's last day on this earth, November 17, 1951, her face was radiant with light. When she uttered her last words, a big smile illumined her face and she exclaimed, "What joy! What joy! Too much, too much joy!" Within an hour, she had left.

Although her guru, Yogananda Paramahamsa, had been told by the Divine Mother never to be in the room when one of his devotees died, he was immersed in deep meditation nearby during the final stages of Gyanamata's dying process. He arrived at her side shortly after her departure. After spending some time alone with her body, offering his blessings, he motioned a few disciples into the room. The master asked them to feel the temperature of her feet—which was very cold. Then he had them feel the top of her head, which was extremely hot, as if on fire. The master explained: "This shows she has left the body in the highest state of *samadhi*. Her soul departed through the highest spiritual center, the thousand-petaled lotus in the brain. Now she has achieved that final state of *mukti* [liberation]; she is free. She has no need to return to the world. But we will meet again." Later the master told his disciples, "You must know that her passing symbolizes that I will be leaving this world shortly." Less than four months later, Yogananda Paramahamsa left his body.

↫ 89 ↬

In 1943, at the age of sixty-six, Seki Seisetsu became the head of all the Rinzai temples in Japan. Two years later he became critically ill and on the first of October said to those gathered at his deathbed:

> When I raise my hand, start chanting Shiku Seigan [The Four Vows of the Bodhisattva]. Then at the end, when you hit the *inkin* [small handbell], I will stop breathing. Please do that.

So when Seisetsu Roshi raised his hand, Yamada Mumon Roshi and the two other monks present began chanting, "*Shujo muhen sei gan do...*" and at the end hit the *inkin*. Seeing that

117

Trijang Rinpoche

Seisetsu Roshi's breathing had stopped, within minutes the doctor appeared and gave him an injection to stimulate his heart.

"Not today," Seisetsu Roshi said. Then he added, "Tomorrow, when I raise my hand, you must not give me an injection." He thus forbade the doctor to intervene a second time. On the night of October 2, when Seisetsu Roshi raised his hand, the small group recited the Shiku Seigan again. When the *inkin* was hit, Seisetsu Roshi gave a big yawn, said "Aaaaaah," and breathed his last breath. Those present reported this as being a truly magnificent last moment.

◠ 90 ◠

Trijang Rinpoche summoned his long-time secretary, Palden Tsering, to his bedside on a crisp November morning in 1981. "I shall not be making the trip to Mundgod after all," he announced in a deep, husky voice. Tears came to Palden Tsering's eyes, but he tried to hide them. "Shall I cancel the rail tickets, then?" he asked. The eighty-one-year-old junior tutor to the Dalai Lama did not reply at once, instead he gazed at a *thangka* [Buddhist painting] across the room and fingered his rosary. "Keep them," he replied at last. "I have an appointment there." The following day he died. The Tibetans believe that his next incarnation will be discovered at the South Indian refugee settlement of Mundgod.

◠ 91 ◠

Shortly before he died, Mahatma Gandhi told Manubehn, a close follower: "I wish I might face the assassin's bullets while lying on

119

your lap and repeating the name of Rama with a smile on my face." As he moved through a crowd where he was to speak one January morning in 1948, a man brusquely pushed his way past Manubehn and fired three shots at the Mahatma. "Sri Ram! Sri Ram!" Gandhi said, as he tumbled to the ground.

A monk said to Tozan,
"A monk has died; where has he gone?"
Tozan answered, "After the fire, a sprout of grass"

⌒ 92 ⌒

When Master Tozan was dying a monk said to him, "Master, your four elements are out of harmony, but is there anyone who is never ill?"

"There is," said Tozan.

"Does this one look at you?" asked the monk.

"It is my function to look at him," answered Tozan.

"How about when you yourself look at him?" asked the monk.

"At that moment I see no illness," replied Tozan.

⌒ 93 ⌒

Three months before Bhagawan Nityananda took *mahasamadhi*, a devotee called Mataji from Dadar came to take his *darshan*. The day before she arrived, the master had developed a discharge from his ear. As soon as Mataji learned of this, she began to cry and beg the master not to go away. She interpreted this to be a sign that the master was cleansing his system of toxins, and for only one purpose. The master told her, "Why are you crying? Don't cry. More work is possible in the subtle than in the gross."

Two months before his departure, Bhagawan practically stopped eating. He just drank water or occasionally ate a little fruit. His body became very thin. Even the imploring of the closest devotees could not persuade him to take any food. Doctors were sent for, but Bhagawan was not interested in doctors or drugs. He did not wish to keep the body any longer and no one could compel him to do so. Upon seeing the master's emaciated condition, a devotee asked him, "Baba, it gives me great pain to see your present condition and weak body. Why can't you use your divine power to get over your present condition?" His compassionate answer was, "This body is mere dust and mud. That [power] is not to be used for this. That is only for the devotees."

About 9:30 AM on the morning of his death, a devotee, noticing that Bhagawan's body was very hot, conveyed this to him. Bhagawan replied, "It will be like that," implying that it was the normal condition at that stage. He then repeated words that he had reportedly said often in the last months. "Sadhu became Swami, Swami became Deva to some, Baba and Bhagawan to others; Deva will now enter *samadhi*, constant *samadhi*." These were reportedly Bhagawan's last words, uttered about an hour before entering *mahasamadhi*.

Before his departure, Bhagawan had coffee distributed as *prasad* [gift] to all present. With a smile he gave a fruit to a young

121

boy. A few moments before the end his hands and feet became straight. For some years the joints of his hands and feet had been stiff due to rheumatism; they now became absolutely free. At 10:45 AM the Master took two or three very deep breaths. The last was so deep that his chest became fully expanded. His eyes assumed the *shambhavi mudra*. He cast a look, full of compassion, at the loving devotees all around, and then his eyes turned upwards. The *sushumna* nerve throbbed in the middle of his eyebrows. A melodious sound of Om was heard and his lifebreath was merged in the cosmos.

Bhagawan's body was placed in the lotus posture and placed in the same easy chair in which he normally sat. For two days thousands of devotees gathered to pay homage. On Thursday, amidst the auspicious chanting of Om, some disciples gave his body the holy bath. At 7:30 PM, bedecked with flowers and garlands, Bhagawan was taken to his original home in Ganeshpuri, Vaikunth. After the ground was consecrated, Bhagawan's body was placed on a deerskin seat surrounded by camphor, sandalwood, gold, and jewels. It was placed in the earth forever, to the recitation of the Vedas.

⌐ 94 ⌐

Suzuki Shosan was a samurai until his forty-second year and became a Zen monk in 1620. Wandering from one monastery to another, he spoke and wrote on Buddhist doctrine in a simple style that was understood by all. He often warned against the pursuit of honor and riches. Buddhism, he wrote, is not an abstract doctrine but a way of life: for the warrior, the warrior's way; for the peasant, the peasant's way; for the artisan, the artisan's way; and for the merchant, the merchant's way. A person may choose whatever sect or manner of praying suits him, provided he follows the way with all his heart. As befit a man of samurai status, Shosan emphasized that the most important thing is to "look straight at death. To know death—that is the entire doctrine."

In the spring of 1655 Shosan became ill. When told that his illness was a grave one, he stated that it meant nothing since he had already died more than thirty years before [perhaps meaning when he became a monk]. As his condition became critical his followers gathered around his deathbed. One of them asked him to say "his final words." Shosan looked sharply at the monk and scolded him: "What are you saying? You only show that you don't understand what I've been saying for more than thirty years. Like this, I simply die."

You should strive for a readiness to die!
Be certain and ready; when the time comes,
you will have no fear and no regret.

—Milarepa

⌇ 95 ⌇

Milarepa, considered by many to be Tibet's greatest saint, is said to have knowingly drunk a glass of poison given to him by a jealous

I raise the mirror of my life
Up to my face: sixty years.
With a swing
I smash the reflection—
The world as usual;
all in its place.

—Taigen Sofu
sixteenth-century Zen monk

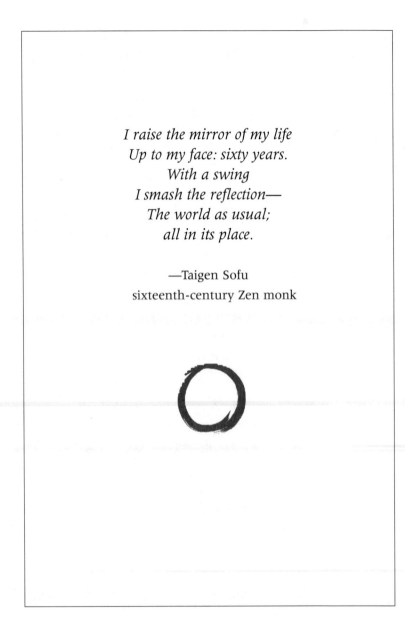

false-admirer. This act of compassion resulted in the culprit totally repenting his action and becoming a disciple. Knowing that he
must soon leave the world, Milarepa sent messages to gather his
disciples and other seekers to him. And to them all Milarepa
preached about Truth. After one talk he said:

> All of you here today are here due to good karma you
> have collected in past lives and now, by being together,
> there is a certain pure and holy bond between us... I
> implore you to remember my discourse and to put the
> teachings into practice in your daily lives to the best of
> your abilities. If you do, then in whatever realm I may
> arrive at the Perfection of Buddhahood you shall be the
> first to receive the Truth I shall teach. Take comfort in this
> thought.

Some days later when a disciple wanted to intercede with the
Powers on his behalf, Milarepa replied that illness in a yogi
should be a spur to drive him on and prayers should not be
offered for his recovery; he should use his illness to progress spir-
itually and ever be ready for suffering and even death. He went
on: "The time has come when the body that is mind-evolved only
must become merged into the Realm of Light and no rites are
necessary for this."

When asked by his disciples about funeral instructions,
Milarepa replied:

> ...Instead of erecting stupas, cultivate a loving devotion to
> all parts of the Dharma and set up the Banner of Love,
> and in place of memorials let there be daily prayers... Life
> is short, the moment of death unknown to you, so apply
> yourselves to meditation.

125

Milarepa then took up residence at Chubar and his illness increased. When two of his leading disciples asked him to what realm he was going and where they should direct their prayers to him, he responded: "Direct your prayers wherever you feel it best; wherever you pray, as long as you are sincere and in earnest, I shall be there with you. So pray earnestly and unwaveringly. I am going to the Realm of Happiness first of all." Then Milarepa sang his two disciples a song, after which he seemed to sink into a trance from which he never awoke. He died at age eighty-four in the year 1135.

ᚖ 96 ᚖ

Just before Master Kassan was about to die he called the chief monk and said, "I have preached the Way to the monks for many years. The profound meaning of Buddhism is to be known by each person himself. My illusory life is over, I am about to depart. You monks should go on just the same as when I was alive. You should not blindly make ordinary people miserable." Having said this, he immediately passed away.

ᚖ 97 ᚖ

During His Holiness the Sixteenth Karmapa's final visit to America in 1980, it was announced that he had a serious form of cancer. His final eighteen days were spent in an Illinois hospital, during which time his disciples reported that "His Holiness remained extremely cheerful. His spontaneous activity of benefiting beings never ceased."

The Sixteenth Karmapa

Shortly before his death on November 5, 1981, a western disciple went in pay his final respects. When he put his head down to receive his blessing, he found himself breaking into uncontrollable tears. As the tears continued to flow, the Karmapa gently touched his hair. When he stopped crying, he raised his head to find the Karmapa looking directly into his eyes. With a slight smile on his face, he said to the disciple, "Nothing happens." These words, so simple and so unaffected, thrust the profound truth of impermanence once again into the disciple's being.

The Karmapa's attending doctor, also a westerner, was amazed at how his patient never complained of pain, or even looked in pain. Even more astounding to him, from a medical viewpoint, was the fact that for twenty-four, forty-eight, and even up to seventy-two hours after death, the Karmapa's heart was still warm to the touch. He remarked, "As a physician, I have no explanation for this." However, according to the Tibetan tradition, this is a sign of *samadhi*. Upon the request of his followers, the Illinois hospital gave permission—probably for the first time in its history—for the body to stay in the hospital room for two days, so that sacred rituals could be performed. Situ Rinpoche bathed the body and drew protective mantras on it, and the monks began performing *pujas* [rituals] outside the room.

The Karmapa's body was flown to Rumtek, his monastery in Sikkim. There it was prepared for cremation in the traditional manner—seated upright in the meditation posture, wrapped in gauze and brocade—and seated in a special room. A wide range of people came to pay their respects. Preparations began immediately to construct a special shrine, or *chorten*—said to symbolically represent the body, speech, and mind of enlightenment—to contain the body of the Karmapa during the cremation ceremony. During the seven intervening weeks, purification ceremonies were performed continuously and prayers were offered for the Karmapa's speedy reincarnation for the sake of all sentient beings. As people arrived by the thousands, representing all sects of Buddhism, each filed past the shrine to pay their respects and make the traditional offering of a white silk scarf. As the cremation fire was about to be lit, a rainbow appeared above the monastery in the clear, blue sky.

As the fire was burning, a few members of the documentary film crew reported seeing an explosion from the top of the *chorten*. One member saw something black fly up into the air, which did not come down. Later one of the rinpoches explained that this object was the top of His Holiness' skull; that the *dakinis* [goddesses that transmute suffering] had been waiting in air above the monastery to welcome His Holiness and this was a sign that he had gone to meet them and be with them.

How wonderful! The waves of individual selves
according to their nature rise up, playing for a time,
and disappear. I remain the shoreless ocean.
—from the *Ashtavakra Samhita*

☞ 98 ☜

On the day before he died, the seventy-six-year-old Zen master Yakuo Tokuken forbade an elaborate funeral and ordered his

Lama Yeshe

students to cremate his body. "Tomorrow morning," he said, " I shall eat rice porridge with your for breakfast, and at noon I shall go." The next day at noon he wrote some last words, threw down his brush, and died sitting upright.

☞ 99 ☜

On the first day of the Tibetan New Year in 1984, Lama Thubten Yeshe's heart surrendered to the enormous pressure it had endured for over ten years. Two faulty valves had enlarged it to twice its normal size. According to modern medicine, it was a miracle he was alive at all. He himself had once said he was alive "only through the power of mantra."

Four months before his passing, it became clear to his disciples how ill he truly was. On January 3, following a fifteen day stay in a Delhi hospital, one of his students fervently requested the lama to live longer. Lama Yeshe agreed he could do so, but "it depends on the karma and hard prayers of the students." A few days later, one of the lama's dearest teachers urged him to allow the cloak of silence about his condition lifted, so that his students could create merit.

By early February it was decided that Lama Yeshe would undergo valve replacement surgery in a California hospital. While waiting for his body to regain enough strength to undergo the surgery, he had a stroke which paralyzed his left side. Specific prayers and mantras found in a Tibetan text were ordered to protect against more paralysis. Although the paralysis did subside, Lama Yeshe's condition grew more critical.

On the eve of his passing, Lama Yeshe was completely conscious, talking and laughing with the nurses and eating strawberries. Around four in the morning Lama Yeshe asked that a particular ritual called the Heruka Sadhana be performed, for which he was able to sit for meditation. Shortly after five in the morning, his heart stopped. Throughout the day, people sat with him reciting mantras. At five in the evening the utter silence of the room was broken by the sudden shouting of Heruka mantras and it was announced: "Now Lama's meditation is finished." This was the first day of the Tibetan New Year—March 3, 1984.

☞ 100 ☜

According to legend, the great Shaivite teacher Abhinavagupta walked into a cave followed by twelve hundred of his disciples, and none of them ever walked out again. The cave, called Bhairava Cave, leads deep into the earth. It exists to this day.

☞ 101 ☜

Chogyam Trungpa Rinpoche was one of the most important figures in the introduction of Tibetan Buddhism to the West. He died in 1987 at the age of 47, but left a lasting legacy in the form of his teachings and the community of students and practitioners that had grown up around him. "Birth and death are expressions of life," he wrote in a statement read after his death. "I have fulfilled my work and conducted my duties as much as the situation allowed, and now I have passed away quite happily... On the whole, discipline and practice are essential, whether I am there or not. Whether you are young or old, you should learn the lesson of impermanence from my death."

Gadge Baba was a wandering saint who carried on the great tradition of Tukaram and Eknath. His name came from the broken piece of earthen pot—*gadge*—he carried on his head. For fifty years he traveled from village to village performing rituals and doing good works. In 1951, his seventy-fifth year, when a friend advised he take rest he replied, "My friend, this body is a hired horse. The more you fondle it, the more docile and lazy it will become. And the more you make it run in the ring, the more it will work for you." Although his continued his traveling, in 1953 he twice fell unconscious from diabetes. Accustomed to sleeping on a mat spread on the earth, when he was hospitalized and made to sleep on a soft mattress in 1956, he escaped. When asked about this, he joked how he was unable to pay a large hospital bill, but then in a more serious tone added that "In the face of God, my case has already come up for hearing. I have gotten a deferment, however, and been allowed to live a few more days." Although quite sick, he continued his travels, with throngs of people following him. On December 7, although his condition was critical, he left Bombay. He died, fittingly, in a van on the way to Nagarwadi. His death was in complete harmony with the life he had lived. Since leaving home at age 29, he had not made any particular place his home. He was a man of the road, and on the road he ended his life. Over three hundred thousand assembled to attend his last rites in Amravati. He often would say the body belonged to the five elements of nature [earth, air, water, sky, and sun] and once its use was over, it had to be returned to the elements.

One Sunday afternoon in late March, 1973, Yasutani Roshi held a
jukai [ceremony to transmit the Buddhist precepts] at Sanun
Zendo in Kamakura, Japan. Having been ill for some time, he sat
down very carefully on the platform, his breath rough and shal-
low. Although he often had a hacking cough, it did not manifest;
after about five minutes his breathing had become composed. He
entered *samadhi* and began the *jukai*. The ceremony was completed without the slightest disturbance, not even a single cough. His
voice was surprisingly loud and strong. Later he said that the day's
jukai would be his last, that he had done it on will-power alone.

Two days later he sat up cross-legged in bed and had his
breakfast of rice gruel. An attendant left to get him a towel, and
when she returned, he had died.

This is one of the last poems Yasutani wrote:

> *Bright, bright, clean, clear, naked and splendid.*
> *The great earth, mountains, and rivers—the uncovered womb.*
> *There are flowers and the moon—who is the Master!*
> *Spring, Autumn, Winter, and Summer compete with new garb.*

The last years of Meher Baba's life were spent mainly in seclusion. From 1925 until his death in 1969 he maintained an unbro-
ken silence, communicating initially with a writing board and
later by signs. He emerged from his final seclusion in July 1968.
In December he began to suffer from muscular spasms of the

Hakuun Ryoko Yasutani

limbs and spine, and he told his *mandali* [group of close companions], "The time is very near." The following month he comforted a devotee who was worried about his health by saying, "All will be well by the end of this month." On December 30, several persons were needed to hold onto his legs as intense spasms shook his body. That evening, although the pain was intense, he told a *mandali* member "I am not this body." Just after noon the following day Baba was seized with a severe spasm and his breathing stopped. Attempts to revive him were unsuccessful. Although a message was sent out to the world that Baba's burial would be February 1, his sister recalled Baba having conveyed by signs on the last morning that "after seven days he would be one hundred percent free." Thus Meher Baba's garlanded body, surrounded by blocks of ice, was left for several days, as a constant flow of devotees poured in to pay their final respects. He was buried on the eighth day. One of his sayings, treasured by his devotees, offered some solace: "When I drop my body, I will remain in all who love me. I can never die. Love me, obey me and you will find me."

Even if death were to fall upon you today like lightning,
you must be ready to die without sadness and regret,
without any residue of clinging for what is left behind.
Remaining in the recognition of the absolute view, you should
leave this life like an eagle soaring up into the blue sky.

—Dilgo Khyentse Rinpoche

At the young age of fifteen, Dilgo Khyentse Rinpoche promised his main teacher just before he passed away that he would unstintingly teach whoever asked him for the Dharma. To prepare for this task, he spent most of the next thirteen years in silent retreat in hermitages and caves in the wilderness near his birthplace in Nepal. After this time, when he told his second teacher he would like to spend the remainder of his life in strict solitary meditation retreat, he received the reply: "The time has come for you to teach and transmit to others all the countless precious teachings you have received." His inner journey had led him to an extraordinary depth of knowledge, which enabled him to be a fountain of loving kindness, wisdom and compassion for all living beings until his death in 1991.

Khyentse Rinpoche was always acutely aware of impermanence and death, and whenever people would ask him to come and visit them, or request him to come again, he would say: "If I am still alive, I shall come." He maintained his characteristic stamina even after having turned eighty. However, in early 1991 he began to show the first signs of ill health while teaching in Bodhgaya, the place where Buddha attained enlightenment, in India. He completed his program there nevertheless, and traveled to Dharamsala where he spent a month giving important teachings to the Dalai Lama. When he returned to Nepal later in the spring, it became obvious that his health was steadily deteriorating. He was losing weight and needed increasingly more rest. Much of his time was passed in silent prayer and meditation; only a few hours of the day were set aside to meet those

Dilgo Khyentse Rinpoche

who most needed to see him. Instead of making another trip to Tibet, he chose instead to spend three and a half months in a sacred retreat site in Bhutan. During this year, he indicated many times that he was going to leave this world soon. He would sometimes joke about it, saying such things as: "Shall I die now?" One time he wrote to a close disciple saying, "We will meet in the Glorious Copper Colored Mountain [the Buddha-field of Padmasambhava, the master who brought Buddhism to Tibet]."

After the retreat in Bhutan, Khyentse Rinpoche seemed to be in better health. He visited several of his disciples who had been in retreat and spoke to them of the ultimate teacher, beyond birth and death or any physical manifestation. He was invited to go to Kalimpong by the Queen Mother of Bhutan, but rather than using the helicopter she had arranged for him, he insisted on doing the strenuous journey by road, to see on the way an old disciple of his.

Shortly after returning to Bhutan, Khyentse Rinpoche again showed signs of illness, and for twelve days was almost completely unable to eat or drink. Four days before passing away, he wrote on a piece of paper: "I shall go on the nineteenth." Two days later his closest disciple and spiritual friend, Trulshik Rinpoche, arrived from Nepal and they had a happy meeting. The day after, September 27, 1991 (the nineteenth of the Tibetan month), at nightfall, he asked his attendants to help him sit in an upright position and went into a peaceful sleep. In the early hours of the morning, his breathing ceased and his mind dissolved in the absolute expanse.

At the request of disciples from Tibet and all over the world, his body was preserved for a year using traditional embalming methods. Every Friday (the day of his death) for the first seven weeks, one hundred thousand butter lamps were offered on the Bodhnath stupa near Shechen Monastery in Nepal. Finally, his remains were cremated near Paro in Bhutan, in November 1992, at a three-day ceremony attended by over a hundred important lamas, the royal family and ministers of Bhutan, five hundred western disciples, and a huge crowd of some fifty thousand devotees—a gathering unprecedented in Bhutan's history. As with other masters, his death was his last teaching, the teaching on impermanence:

> Never forget how swiftly this life will be over—like a flash of summer lightning or the wave of a hand. Now that you have the opportunity to practice the Dharma, do not waste a single moment on anything else, but with all your energy and effort practice the Dharma.

⁊ 106 ⁏

Telanga Swami was a high being who, much to the distress of the Varanasi police, always remained naked. When Telanga Swami realized his mission in this world was fulfilled, he fixed his time of leaving a month before the actual day. On the appointed day, he gave the necessary instructions to his pupils that his body should be enclosed in a wooden chest and cast into the midstream of the Ganges. That day he spent many hours in a closed room in deep meditation. Coming out of the room in the afternoon, he blessed a group of disciples and admirers, assumed the full lotus posture, and attained *mahasamadhi*. He reputedly had attained the age of 280.

When Zen Master Tung-shan felt it was time for him to go, he had his head shaved, took a bath, put on his robe, rang the bell to bid farewell to the community, and sat up till he breathed no more. To all appearances he had died. Thereupon the whole community burst out crying grievously as little children do at the death of their mother. Suddenly the master opened his eyes and said to the weeping monks, "We monks are supposed to be detached from all things transitory. In this consists true spiritual life. To live is to work, to die is to rest. What is the use of groaning and moaning?" He then ordered a "stupidity-purifying" meal for the whole community. After the meal he said to them, "Please make no fuss over me! Be calm as befits a family of monks! Generally speaking, when anyone is at the point of going, he has no use for noise and commotion." Thereupon he returned to the Abbot's room, where he sat in meditation until he passed away.

When the Taoist sage Lai was on the verge of death, another sage asked him, "Great is the Maker of Things! What will become of you now? Where will he send you?" Lai replied, "A child who obeys his father and mother will go wherever they tell him to go—east, west, south, or north. Yin and yang, the elements of nature, are they not to a man like father and mother? If I were not to obey them now that they have brought me to the point of death, how wayward I should be. They are not to be blamed. The great earth burdens me with a body, forces upon me the toil of life, eases me in old age, and calms me in death. If life is good, death is good also. If an ironsmith were casting metal and the metal were to jump up and say, 'Make me into the best of all swords!' the ironsmith would regard it as a bad omen. Now that my human form is decomposing, were I to say,' I want to be a man! Nothing but a man!' the Maker of Things would think me most unworthy. Heaven and earth are a great forge and the Maker of Things is a master ironsmith. Can the place he is sending me to be the wrong place?"

Narrow paths toward the cemetery
generations of abbots
fallen camellias.

—Mitsu Suzuki

AFTERWORD

In his book *Death and Dying: The Tibetan Tradition*, Glenn Mullin remarks: "Nothing is considered to be a more powerful teacher of death and impermanence than the passing of one's own Guru."

I had the great good fortune to be at my master's ashram in India when he passed away. The medical reason Swami Muktananda (affectionately called Baba by his followers) left his body was a heart attack. Several hours before this departure, he began referring to himself in the past tense. No one took special note of this because Siddha Yoga masters, known as "perfected beings," often say mysterious things.

At 11:30 in the evening the ashram gong, normally struck only at sunrise and sunset, began to sound. It seemed odd. In the background the slow drone of chanting could be heard, along with intermittent pounding, like building construction. Since construction by the Indian tribal workers often takes place in the middle of the night, just as weddings can, that seemed less incongruous than the chanting. Down the corridor from the dorm room that I shared with three other women, we heard scurrying footsteps and a young woman's voice whispering, "Baba is sick. Everyone is invited to come chant."

We all threw something on and went quickly downstairs. The chanting and the pounding grew louder—and the situation seemed even more confusing. Why, if Baba was sick, were people tearing out the floor of the meditation room next to his apartment in the courtyard? Wouldn't this disturb him? At that moment, one of the swamis walked up and gently whispered, "Baba left his body." I didn't believe it. He couldn't leave. How could he leave me? Yet, looking around, I saw this was the only sensible explanation. No one would be tearing out the floor unless Baba had left explicit instructions for the preparation of his burial site to begin immediately after his death.

I walked around in a daze. To sit was more painful, so I kept moving. Hundreds of people were now up and about, and each seemed to be encased in a cocoon of shock. Some dropped in limp bundles to the floor to chant, unable to move. Others were vigorously sweeping away dust and debris from the demolition work going on within a few feet of the chanters. The drone of the chant seemed to contain the pain of the universe. I followed what others were doing. First I chanted, and then, when that wasn't right, I swept.

Around 3:00 AM I wandered into Amrit, the coffee shop in the lower garden where Westerners often gathered. At every table stories could be heard about Baba, about his life, about his glory—some going back only a few days, some to fifteen years before. Tears, laughter, disbelief, gratitude. The air was thick with grace. Grace moved in the form of people I thought had limitations. For once, their karmic baggage was suspended, their egos not in view. The limiting concepts that usually gave form to my perception of others—and myself—had dissolved. All I saw was light. Each and every particle of air was illumined.

My mind was totally still. Inside I felt a liquid pool of clear, crystalline light. My heart felt pregnant with the very joy of being alive and present to each second. It was akin to those clear, titillating moments of free-floating adoration one can feel in flashes as an adolescent. But this time the love didn't require an object. It only had to be relished for its own sake; its origin and its destination resided now in the space between my own heartbeats. Each moment was pristine and to be savored simply because it was.

With Baba's *mahasamadhi,* I knew my life was beginning anew. And it all belonged to me, because of him. How can the litany of gratitude ever end for a gift so precious? He is still alive inside of me today. There is only one other gift that can possibly outshine this gift of the Siddha masters: they always leave a living master to continue supporting and guiding their devotees to the final goal. Baba passed on the Siddha lineage to a close disciple he'd been training since she was five-years old, Swami Chidvilasananda—now affectionately known as Gurumayi.

Two summers ago while I was visiting Gurumayi at Shree Muktananda Ashram in South Fallsburg, New York, I took a course entitled "Does Death Really Exist?" One late afternoon around the middle of the course, a lovely woman swami asked us all to close our eyes for a contemplation. She said: "Ask yourself, 'Where is it that I am going to go when I die?'" Before the question was out of her mouth, I heard words resounding inside my chest: "In Baba's heart." These words had clearly been formulated by something other than my conscious mind. I left the Catskills that summer with a new joy that came from a sense of knowing where I was ultimately going to reside.

For some mysterious reason, when I got home I started collecting death stories of masters and keying them into my computer. A book seemed to be in the making.

My original title for it, *Diamond Light: How Great Beings Die,* arose from an experience following my mother's death. During the last several of her eighty-nine years, she never wanted us to buy her presents, but would always relish resting her eyes on the radiant diamonds in the jewelry stores at the mall when we went out to lunch. The diamond in her wedding ring had been flawed for over half a century and a yearning seemed to be there.

She died peacefully the day before Valentine's Day in 1993, one week after suffering a heart attack. The following Sunday during our morning meditation, I had a strong vision. She appeared standing next to Baba's guru, Bhagawan Nityananda, ecstatically waving her arms, with an expression of indescribable joy on her face. Behind her, I saw what looked like a huge icicle. Then I heard her utter, almost in a cheer, "He gave me diamonds! He gave me diamonds!" For me, this was a confirmation that Bhagawan had given her the inner light, the true gem for which she had been yearning.

A few years later, in August 1995, my ninety-three-year-old father came to spend the last two weeks of his life in our home. Although he had not shown any interest in my yogic practices over the years, the one thing Dad did enjoy was listening to my tape of Baba chanting *Om Namah Shivaya*, the initiation mantra of the Siddha Yoga lineage. A few days before he left he wanted me to explain to him very simply who Baba Muktananda was. I told him Baba was a man who had spent his entire life looking for God and that, under the guidance of his master, he had attained God-realization, he had become one with God. This seemed to answer his question.

About three hours before he died, I asked Dad if he wanted me to play the tape of Baba chanting the mantra. I was very surprised to hear his response, which turned out to be his final words: "Just until He comes. Just until He comes." I'm not sure exactly what he meant by this, but I experienced the words as a gift; they made me feel a deep joy inside. I knew whatever form "He" was going to come in, it would be just perfect.

Being present at my dad's death was perhaps the most intimate experience I ever had with him. It felt like a sacred honor and privilege that he allowed me to partake in his departure. The Siddha lineage teaches that all family members of devotees for seven generations receive the grace and protection of the Siddha masters. The way my parents were so clearly taken care of gave me an insight into the truth and beauty of this teaching.

The palpable grace I experienced around their dying process and departure inspired a revised title for this book—*Graceful Exits*—that emerged very naturally during a quiet moment. Still, when people would ask why I was compiling the book, I couldn't answer. I didn't know. The underlying reason, about which I had no conscious awareness, only became clear several weeks ago. I felt some chest pain and walked into our nearby emergency room thinking I was having a mild heart attack. Five hours later I walked out, having learned I had advanced lung cancer metastasized to bone. The window on my life had become very short. I had, unknowingly, been busy compiling a training manual for my own "graceful exit!"

Upon hearing this news, I turned again to the source that had always nourished me: my guru. As soon as I sent the message to Gurumayi, my perception of the world began to shift radically. Suddenly I could see karmic blocks that had veiled my consciousness this entire lifetime. Many gifts of sublime insight and understanding about life, and death, were showered upon me. One morning in meditation I had an incredible vision. I saw Gurumayi's face close up, lying on the ground. Her eyes opened, and she gave me a big smile. "I am with you," she said. That faded, and then I saw the same scene, only now her face was totally translucent, and I heard the words, "Sushila, I am dying with you." Then she went on to answer a big practical question I had about the time between now and leaving. "Die a little bit each day in meditation," she said. This experience was the most extraordinary gift and planted in me the knowledge that Gurumayi will be with me every minute of this path and will be there to take me across.

One month after hearing the news, on my tenth and final day of palliative brain radiation, I was able to journey to South Fallsburg to be with Gurumayi in person for a few weeks. I started experiencing even greater levels of Gurumayi's compassion in my heart. I arrived with digestive troubles, the side effects of radiation. Gurumayi came in meditation and told me "Offer your food to me and I will turn it to *prana*, to light." After that I would do this at each meal and the food went down like nectar. During this time, the profound insights and understandings I had been given seemed to settle deep inside, and I was catapulted into a state of simply being present in the heart. It was a fearless state, without desire. So when I was asked to give a talk in the meditation intensive to more than a thousand people, not even a ripple of anxiety arose. (Quite unusual, given that throughout my twenty-some years of Siddha Yoga I secretly harbored an intense fear of being confronted with such a request.) Instead, because of the state of grace that I had been granted, the delivery of the talk was a joyful offering, a natural and comfortable sharing with my Self. When I mentioned in the talk that we were all in this process (of dying) together, there was a brief hush in the room. That was immediately broken by a peal of laughter when I added that someone told me I was simply doing "advance work" for all the devotees.

Now, back home, the grace keeps flowing. I experience the full support of my guru and the entire Siddha community each day as my journey continues. I might even say I'm looking forward to my dying experience as it continues to unveil itself each day. In one meditation I had before going to Fallsburg, Gurumayi told me to recall the most profound and extraordinary meditations I'd had over the past twenty years. Then she said the "mahameditation," the supreme meditation, was unimaginably beyond any of these experiences.

If this book serves to make the departure of even one other person more grace-filled, more filled with light, more saturated with God's sublime love and understanding, it will have more than served its purpose.

Sushila Blackman
September 21, 1996

☙ ❧

Sushila Blackman died peacefully and consciously on the afternoon of Saturday, November 9, 1996. In the spiritual tradition she followed, this day is celebrated as Diwali, the Festival of Lights, and the beginning of the New Year.

MASTERS AND SOURCES

The following is a list of the masters whose death stories are recounted in this book and the original sources from which the stories were drawn. The masters' names are followed by their life dates (when available) and the religious tradition to which they belonged. Names are rendered as per the source material, which means, for example, that names of some Chinese masters have been given Japanese readings, and there are some inconsistencies in romanization. Ch'an is the Chinese pronunciation of the character pronounced Zen in Japanese, and has been used to identify Chinese masters in that tradition.

1. Anonymous Buddhist master.
   From *What Survives? Contemporary Explorations of Life After Death,* edited by Gary Doore (New York: Tarcher/Putnam, 1990).
2. Matsuo Basho (1644–94). Zen.
   From *Zen Poems of China and Japan* by Lucien Stryk, Takashi Ikemoto, and Taigan Takayama. Copyright ©1973 by Lucien Stryk, Takashi Ikemoto, and Taigan Takayama. Used by permission of Doubleday, a division of Bantam Doubleday Dell Publishing Group, Inc.
3. Taji (1889–1953). Zen.
   From *The Wheel of Life and Death* by Philip Kapleau. Copyright © 1989 by the Rochester Zen Center. Used by permission of Doubleday, a division of Bantam Doubleday Dell Publishing Group, Inc.
4. Neem Karoli Baba (20th c.). Hindu.
   From *Miracle of Love: Stories of Neem Karoli Baba* by Ram Dass (Santa Fe: Hanuman Foundation, 1979). By permission.
5. Takuan Soho (1573–1645). Zen.
   From *The Wheel of Death* by Philip Kapleau, ©1971. Reprinted by arrangement with the Rochester Zen Center.
6. Anandamayi Ma (1896–1982). Hindu.
   Elizabeth Hallstrom, "My Mother, My God: Anandamayi Ma" (Ph.D. dissertation, Harvard University, 1995).

7. Hakuin Ekaku (1689–1769). Zen.
   John Stevens, *Three Zen Masters: Ikkyu, Hakuin, and Ryokan* (Tokyo: Kodansha International, 1993). By permission.
8. Lama Tseten (20th c.). Tibetan.
   From *The Tibetan Book of Living and Dying* by Sogyal Rinpoche. Copyright ©1993 by Rigpa Fellowship. By permission.
9. Akkalkot Swami (dates unknown). Hindu.
   From an unpublished MS in the Shree Muktananda Ashram library, South Fallsburg, NY, and from N.S. Karandikar, *Biography of Sri Swami Samarth Akkalkot Maharaj* (Bombay: P.B. Paanjpe, n.d.).
10. Tenno Dogo (J. for T'ien-huang Tao-wu; 748–807). Ch'an.
    From *The Wheel of Death* by Philip Kapleau, ©1971. Reprinted by arrangement with the Rochester Zen Center.
11. The Buddha (563–483 BC).
    From *Death and Dying: The Tibetan Tradition* by Glen H. Mullin (London: Penguin Arkana, 1987). Copyright © 1986 Glenn H. Mullin. By permission.
12. Lin-chi I-hsüan (d. 866). Ch'an.
    From *Samadhi* by Mike Sayama. By permission of the State University of New York Press ©1986).
13. Kalu Rinpoche (1904–89). Tibetan.
    From *The Tibetan Book of Living and Dying* by Sogyal Rinpoche. Copyright ©1993 by Rigpa Fellowship. By permission.
14. Chuang Tzu (369–286 BC). Taoist.
    From *The Wheel of Death* by Philip Kapleau, ©1971. Reprinted by arrangement with the Rochester Zen Center.
15. Razan (9th c). Ch'an.
    From *The Wheel of Death* by Philip Kapleau, ©1971. Reprinted by arrangement with the Rochester Zen Center.
16. Sri Ramakrishna (1836–86). Hindu.
    From *Saints of India* by Anna (Madras: Sri Ramakrishna Math, 1977); and from *Gurus, Swamis, Avatars* by Marvin Henry Harper (Philadelphia: Westminster Press, 1972). By permission.
17. Sarada Devi (1853–1920). Hindu.
    From *Great Women of India* by Ramesh Majundar (Almora, India: Mayavati, 1982).
18. Hui Neng (638–713). Ch'an.
    Heinrich Dumoulin, *Zen Buddhism: A History,* vol. 1, *India and China.* (New York: Macmillan, 1988).
19. Sonam Namgyal (1873–1952). Tibetan.
    From *The Tibetan Book of Living and Dying* by Sogyal Rinpoche. Copyright ©1993 by Rigpa Fellowship. By permission.
20. Hofuku Juten (J. for Pao-fu Ts'ung-chan; d. 928). Ch'an.
    From *The Wheel of Death* by Philip Kapleau, © 1971. Reprinted by arrangement with the Rochester Zen Center.

21. Sai Baba (d. 1918). Hindu.

From *The Life and Teachings of Sai Baba of Shirdi* by Antonio Rigopoulos. By permission of the State University of New York Press, ©1993.

22. Venkusha (19th c.) Hindu.

From *The Life and Teachings of Sai Baba of Shirdi* by Antonio Rigopoulos. By permission of the State University of New York Press, ©1993.

23. Bassui Tokusho (1327–87). Zen.

From *Mud and Water: A Collection of Talks by the Zen Master Bassui,* translated by Arthur Braverman (San Francisco: North Point Press, 1989).

24. Yamamoto Gempo (1865–1961). Zen.

From *The Wheel of Death* by Philip Kapleau, © 1971. Reprinted by arrangement with the Rochester Zen Center.

25. Nyogen Senzaki (1876–1958). Zen.

From *Crazy Clouds: Zen Radicals, Rebels & Reformers* by Perle Besserman and Manfred Stegner (Boston; Shambala, 1991); and *Nine-Headed Dragon River* by Peter Matthiesen, (Boston: Shambala, 1985).

26. Ramana Maharshi (1879–1950). Hindu.

From *Ten Saints of India* by T.M.P. Mahadevan (Bombay: Bharatiya Vidya Bhavan, 1971).

27. Kabir (1440–1518). Hindu/Muslim.

From *Sufis, Mystics, and Yogis of India* by Bankey Behari (Bombay: Bharatiya Vidya Bhavan, 1962); and *Spiritual Masters from India* by Shashi Ahluwalia (Delhi: Manas Publications, 1987).

28. Yakusan Igen (J. for Yüeh-shan Wei-yen; 751–843). Ch'an.

From *The Wheel of Death* by Philip Kapleau, © 1971. Reprinted by arrangement with the Rochester Zen Center.

29. Swami Ram Tirth (1873–1906). Hindu.

From *Spiritual Masters from India* by Shashi Ahluwalia (Delhi: Manas Publications, 1987); and from *Practical Vedanta of Swami Ram Tirth,* edited by Brandt Dayton (Honesdale, PA: The Himalayan International Institute, 1978).

30. Former abbot of Namgyal Dratsang. Tibetan.

From *Death and Dying: The Tibetan Tradition* by Glen H. Mullin (London: Penguin Arkana, 1987). Copyright © 1986 Glenn H. Mullin. By permission.

31. Shunryu Suzuki (1905–71). Zen.

From *Zen Mind, Beginner's Mind* by Shunryu Suzuki (New York: Weatherhill, 1970).

32. First Dalai Lama (Gendün Drub; 1391–1475). Tibetan.

From *Death and Dying: The Tibetan Tradition* by Glen H. Mullin (London: Penguin Arkana, 1987). Copyright © 1986 Glenn H. Mullin. By permission.

33. Gauribai (dates unknown). Hindu.

From *Women Saints of East and West* (Hollywood, CA: Vedanta Press, 1978). By permission.

34. Tekisui (1822–99). Zen.
From *Zen: Poems, Sermons, Anecdotes, Interviews,* translated by Lucien Stryk and Takashi Ikemoto (Athens, OH: Ohio University Press/Swallow Press, 1981). By permission.

35. Shriman Tapasviji Maharaj (d. 1955). Hindu.
From *Maharaj* by T.S. Anantha Murthy, (San Raphael, CA: Dawn Horse Press, 1986). By permission.

36. Gaurima (1858–1938). Hindu.
From *Women Saints of East and West* (Hollywood, CA: Vedanta Press, 1978). By permission.

37. Shri Bodhendra (d. 1692). Hindu.
From *Saints of the Cauvery Delta* by R. Krishnamurthy (New Delhi: Concept, 1979).

38. Ling Mo (d. 818). Ch'an.
From *Transmission of the Lamp: Early Masters.* Compiled by Tao Yuan, translated by Sohaku Ogata. (Wolfeboro, NH: Longwood Academic Press, 1990).

39. Sadsiva Brahmendra (18th c.). Hindu.
From *Saints of the Cauvery Delta* by R. Krishnamurthy (New Delhi: Concept, 1979).

40. Maharshi Brahmanda (d. 1906). Hindu.
From *Splendor in the Cave* by S. Banerjee, (Banerjee Publishing, 1976); and *Saints of the Cauvery Delta* by R. Krishnamurthy (New Delhi: Concept, 1979).

41. Nan Ch'uan (748–835). Ch'an.
From *Transmission of the Lamp: Early Masters.* Compiled by Tao Yuan, translated by Sohaku Ogata. (Wolfeboro, NH: Longwood Academic Press, 1990).

42. Shen Tsan (dates unknown). Ch'an.
From *Transmission of the Lamp: Early Masters.* Compiled by Tao Yuan, translated by Sohaku Ogata. (Wolfeboro, NH: Longwood Academic Press, 1990).

43. Retreat master at Kham (20th c.). Tibetan.
From *The Tibetan Book of Living and Dying* by Sogyal Rinpoche. Copyright ©1993 by Rigpa Fellowship. By permission.

44. Yin Feng (9th c.). Zen.
From *Transmission of the Lamp: Early Masters.* Compiled by Tao Yuan, translated by Sohaku Ogata. (Wolfeboro, NH: Longwood Academic Press, 1990).

45. Dasui Fazhen (10th c.) Ch'an.
From *A Zen Life: D.T. Suzuki Remembered,* edited by Masao Abe (New York: Weatherhill, 1986).

46. Kyabje Ling Rinpoche (d. 1983). Tibetan.
Story courtesy of Jhampa Shaneman, B.A.S.I.S., Duncan, British Columbia.

47. Tao-ch'o (dates unknown). Chinese Buddhist.
From *Breaking the Circle: Death and Afterlife in Buddhism* by Carl B. Becker (Carbondale, IL: Southern Illinois University Press, 1993). By permission.

48. Seng-chi (dates unknown). Chinese Buddhist.
   From *Breaking the Circle: Death and Afterlife in Buddhism* by Carl B. Becker
   (Carbondale, IL: Southern Illinois University Press, 1993). By permission.
49. Ikkyu Sojun (1394–1481). Zen.
   From *Three Zen Masters: Ikkyu, Hakuin, and Ryokan* by John Stevens (Tokyo:
   Kodansha International, 1993). By permission.
50. Swami Vivekananda (1863–1902). Hindu.
   From *Vivekananda: A Biography* by Swami Nikhilananda (Calcutta: Advaita
   Ashram, 1953).
51. Jetsunla (d. 1959?). Tibetan.
   From *Tibetan Buddhist Nuns* by Hanna Navnevik, (Oslo: Norwegian
   University Press, 1989).
52. Hakuyu Taizan Maezumi (1931–95). Zen.
   Death story and poem courtesy of the White Plum Sangha.
53. Hui-yung (d. 414). Chinese Buddhist.
   From *Breaking the Circle: Death and Afterlife in Buddhism* by Carl B. Becker
   (Carbondale, IL: Southern Illinois University Press, 1993). By permission.
54. Bankei Eitaku (1622–93). Zen.
   From *Crazy Clouds: Zen Radicals, Rebels & Reformers* by Perle Besserman and
   Manfred Stegner (Boston; Shambala, 1991).
55. P'ang Yun (740–808). Ch'an.
   From *Crazy Clouds: Zen Radicals, Rebels & Reformers* by Perle Besserman and
   Manfred Stegner (Boston; Shambala, 1991).
56. Lahiri Mahasaya (1828–95). Hindu.
   From *Autobiography of a Yogi* by Paramahamsa Yogananda (Los Angeles: Self-
   Realization Fellowship, 1946). By permission.
57. Chih-hsien (d. 905). Ch'an.
   Nancy Wilson Ross, *The World of Zen* (New York: Random House, 1960).
58. Ryoen Genseki (dates uknown). Zen.
   From *Samadhi* by Mike Sayama. By permission of the State University of
   New York Press ©1986).
59. Dokyo Etan (1642–1721). Zen.
   From *Samadhi* by Mike Sayama. By permission of the State University of
   New York Press ©1986).
60. Daito Kokushi (1282–1337). Zen.
   From *Samadhi* by Mike Sayama. By permission of the State University of
   New York Press ©1986).
61. Kwaisen (d. 1582). Zen.
   From *Samadhi* by Mike Sayama. By permission of the State University of
   New York Press ©1986).
62. Eshun (dates unknown). Zen
   From *Zen Flesh, Zen Bones: A Collection of Zen and Pre-Zen Writings,* edited by
   Paul Reps (New York: Doubleday, 1957).

63. Fugai (1779–1847). Zen.
From *The Wheel of Death* by Philip Kapleau, © 1971. Reprinted by arrangement with the Rochester Zen Center.

64. Swami Brahmananda (1863–1922). Hindu.
From *The Eternal Companion: Brahmananda, His Life and Teachings* by Swami Prabhavananda (Hollywood, CA: The Vedanta Press, 1960). By permission.

65. Paramahansa Yogananda (1853–1952). Hindu.
Paramahansa Yogananda: In Memorium (Los Angeles: Self-Realization Fellowship, undated pamphlet). By permission.

66. Nampo Shomyo (Daio Kokushi; 1235–1308). Zen.
Lucien Stryk, Takashi Ikemoto, and Taigan Takayama, *Zen Poems of China and Japan* (New York: Doubleday, 1973); Mike Sayama, *Samadhi* (Albany: State University of New York Press, 1986).By permission.

67. Kanzan Egen (1277–1360). Zen.
From *Samadhi* by Mike Sayama. By permission of the State University of New York Press ©1986.

68. Daibai (Daibai Hojo, J. for Ta-mei Fa-ch'ang; 752–839). Ch'an.
From *Zen Poems of China and Japan* by Lucien Stryk, Takashi Ikemoto, and Taigan Takayama. Copyright ©1973 by Lucien Stryk, Takashi Ikemoto, and Taigan Takayama. Used by permission of Doubleday, a division of Bantam Doubleday Dell Publishing Group, Inc.

69. Etsugan (1616–1681). Zen.
From *Zen: Poems, Sermons, Anecdotes, Interviews,* translated by Lucien Stryk and Takashi Ikemoto (Athens, OH: Ohio University Press/Swallow Press, 1981). By permission.

70. P'u-hua (d. 860). Ch'an.
From *The Laughing Buddha: Zen and the Comic Spirit* by Conrad Hyers (Wolfeboro, NH: Longwood Academic Press, 1989).

71. Jamyang Khyentse (1892–1959). Tibetan.
From *The Tibetan Book of Living and Dying* by Sogyal Rinpoche. Copyright ©1993 by Rigpa Fellowship. By permission.

72. Hyma (20th c.). Hindu.
Linda Johnsen, *Daughters of the Goddess: The Women Saints of India* (Yes International Publishers, 1994). By permission.

73. Guru Nanak (1469–1539). Sikh.
Harbans Singh, *Guru Nanak and the Origins of the Sikh Path* (Bombay: Asia Publishing House, 1969).

74. Xu Yun (1840–1959). Ch'an.
From *The Empty Cloud: The Autobiography of the Chinese Zen Master Xu Yun.* Translated by Charles Luk (Rockport, MA: Element Books, 1988). By permission.

75. Yamaoka Tesshu (1836–88). Zen.
From *The Sword of No-Sword* by John Stevens (Boston: Shambala, 1984).

76. Sri Aurobindo (1872–1950). Hindu.
From *The Passing of Sri Aurobindo: Its Inner Significance and Consequence* by K.D.
Sethna (Pondicherry, India: Sri Aurobindo Ashram, 1951); and from Peter
Heehs, *Sri Aurobindo* (Oxford: Oxford University Press, 1989). By permission.

77. Kukai (Kobo Daishi; 774–835). Shingon sect of Japanese Buddhism.
From *Kukai: Major Works,* edited by Yoshito S. Hakeda. Copyright ©1972 by
Columbia University Press. Reprinted with permission of the publisher.

78. Shivapuri Baba (d. 20th c.). Hindu.
From *Long Pilgrimage: The Life and Teachings of Sri Govindananda Bharati* by
J.G. Bennett (London: Hodder and Stoughton, 1965).

79. Tsong Khapa (1357–1419). Tibetan.
From *The Life and Teachings of Tsong Khapa,* edited by Robert Thurman
(Dharamsala, India: Library of Tibetan Works and Archives, 1993).

80. Eisai (1141–1215). Zen.
From *Japanese Death Poems,* edited by Yoel Hoffman. (Tokyo: Charles E.
Tuttle, 1986). By permission.

81. Ninakawa (15th c.). Zen.
From *Zen Flesh, Zen Bones,* edited by Paul Reps (New York: Doubleday, 1957).

82. Jalaluddin Rumi (1207–73). Sufi.
From *Legends of the Sufis: Selected Anecdotes,* translated by J.W. Redhouse
(Wheaton, IL: Theosophical Publishing House, Ltd., 1976). Reprinted by per-
mission of the Theosophical Society, London.

83. Swami Sivananda (1887–1963). Hindu.
Sivananda: Biography of a Modern Sage, vol. 1 (Sivanandanagar, India: Divine
Life Trust Society, 1985).

84. Goei (dates unknown). Zen.
R.H. Blyth, *Zen and Zen Classics,* vol. 2 (Tokyo: Hokuseido Press, 1964).

85. Enni Ben'en (1201–80). Zen.
From *Japanese Death Poems,* edited by Yoel Hoffman. (Tokyo: Charles E.
Tuttle, 1986). By permission.

86. Yü. Legendary Taoist master.
From *Japanese Death Poems,* edited by Yoel Hoffman. (Tokyo: Charles E.
Tuttle, 1986). By permission.

87. Nogami Senryo (1883–1980). Zen.
Paula Arai, "Women Living Zen: Soto Buddhist Nuns in Japan" (unpublished MS, 1996). By permission.

88. Gyanamata (d. 1951). Hindu.
From *God Alone: The Life and Letters of a Saint* by Sri Yanamata, (Los Angeles:
Self-Realization Fellowship, 1984).

89. Seki Seisetsu (1876–1945). Zen.
From *Omori Sogen: The Art of a Zen Master.* (London: Kegan Paul International,
forthcoming).

90. Trijang Rinpoche (1900–81). Tibetan.
From *The Last Dalai Lama* by Michael H. Goodman, ©1986. Reprinted by arrangement with Shambala Publications, Inc., Boston, MA.

91. Mahatma Gandhi (1869–1948). Hindu.
From *The Sacred Art of Dying* by Paul Kramer. Copyright ©1988 by the Paulist Press. By permission.

92. Tozan Ryokai (J. for Tung-shan Liang-chieh; 807–69). Ch'an.
From *The Wheel of Death* by Philip Kapleau, © 1971. Reprinted by arrangement with the Rochester Zen Center.

93. Bhagawan Nityananda (d. 1961). Hindu.
From *Nityananda: The Divine Presence* by M.U. Hatengei (Cambridge, MA: Rudra Press, 1984). By permission.

94. Suzuki Shosan (1578–1655). Zen.
From *Japanese Death Poems,* edited by Yoel Hoffman. (Tokyo: Charles E. Tuttle, 1986). By permission.

95. Milarepa (1052–1135). Tibetan.
W.Y. Evans-Wentz, trans., *The Life of Milarepa: Tibet's Great Yogi* (Oxford: Oxford University Press, 1962).

96. Kassan (dates unknown). Zen.
From *The Wheel of Death* by Philip Kapleau, © 1971. Reprinted by arrangement with the Rochester Zen Center.

97. Sixteenth Karmapa (Rigpe Dorje; 1924–81). Tibetan.
Centre Productions, Inc., *The Lion's Roar* (video; Boulder, CO: Nalanda Foundation, 1985). By permission.

98. Yakuo Tokuken (1244–1320). Zen.
From *Japanese Death Poems,* edited by Yoel Hoffman. (Tokyo: Charles E. Tuttle, 1986). By permission.

99. Lama Thubten Yeshe (1935–84).
Lori de Aratanha and Robina Courtin, "Lama Thubten Yeshe, 1935–84," in *Mandala* (newsletter of FPMT, Soquel, CA, nd.). By permission.

100. Abinavagupta (dates unknown). Hindu.
From an unknown oral source.

101. Chogyam Trungpa Rinpoche (1940–87). Tibetan.
From *How the Swans Came to the Lake: A Narrative History of Buddhism in America* by Rick Fields, ©1992. Reprinted by arrangement with Shambala Publications, Inc.,Boston, MA

102. Gadge Baba (d. 1956). Hindu.
Vasant Shirwadkar, *The Wandering Saint: The Life and Teachings of Gadge Baba* (Bombay: Sri Gadge Baba Prakashan Samiti, n.d.)

103. Hakuun Ryoko Yasutani (1885–1973). Zen.
From the "Yasutani Roshi Memorial Issue," *ZCLA Journal,* Summer/Fall 1973. By permission of the Zen Center of Los Angeles.

104. Meher Baba (1894–1969). Hindu.
    From *Much Silence: Meher Baba and His Work,* by Tom and Dorothy Hopkinson (Bombay: Meher House Publications, 1981).
105. Dilgo Khyentse Rinpoche (1910–91). Tibetan.
    Story courtesy Mattieu Ricard. ©1996 by the Padmakara Translation Group.
106. Telanga Swami (d. 20th c.). Hindu.
    From *Saints and Sages of India* by Manu G. Bhagat, (n.p.: Mungshiram Manoharlal, 1976).
107. Tung-shan (807–69). Ch'an.
    From *The Golden Age of Zen* by John C.H. Wu (Taipei, Taiwan: United Publishing Center, 1975).
108. Lai. Legendary Taoist master.
    From *Japanese Death Poems,* edited by Yoel Hoffman. (Tokyo: Charles E. Tuttle, 1986). By permission.

POETRY

Death poems on pages 35, 50, 58, 66, and 124 from *Japanese Death Poems,* edited by Yoel Hoffman. (Tokyo: Charles E. Tuttle, 1986). By permission.

Death poems on pages 77, 84, and 108 from *Zen Poems of China and Japan* by Lucien Stryk, Takashi Ikemoto, and Taigan Takayama. Copyright ©1973 by Lucien Stryk, Takashi Ikemoto, and Taigan Takayama. Used by permission of Doubleday, a division of Bantam Doubleday Dell Publishing Group, Inc.

Poem on page 142 from *Essential Zen,* edited by Kazuaki Tanahashi and Tensho David Schneider (San Francisco: HarperSanFrancisco, 1994). By permission.

PHOTO CREDITS

Sivananda (p. 111). Reproduced with permission of The International Sivananda Yoga Vedanta Centre, Quebec, Canada.

Nogami Senryo (p. 113). Reproduced with permission of Seikanji Temple, Nagoya, Japan.

Trijang Rinpoche (p. 118). Reproduced with permission of *Mandala* (Soquel, CA), courtesy of Jaffa Elias.

16th Karmapa (p. 127). Photo by Sanje Elliott. Reproduced with permission.

Lama Yeshe (p. 130). Photo by Jonathan Landaw. Reproduced with permission from *Introduction to Tantra* (Boston: Wisdom Publications, 1978).

Yasutani Roshi (p. 135). Reproduced from *A Zen Wave: Basho's Haiku and Zen* by Robert Aitken (New York: Weatherhill, 1978).

Dilgo Khyentse Rinpoche (p. 138). Photo by Matthieu Ricard. Reproduced with permission.

Front cover: The meditating monk is a detail from a photograph by André Jewell (Bijoux), from his forthcoming book *Zanskar Journeys*. Reproduced with permission.

The "weathermark" identifies this book as a production of Weatherhill, Inc., publishers of fine books on Asia and the Pacific. Editorial supervision and book design: D.S. Noble. Cover design by Sushila Blackman and D.S. Noble. Production supervision: Bill Rose. Printed and bound by Quebecor. The typeface used is Meridien, with Charlemagne for display.